SHARK TANK
JUMP START YOUR BUSINESS

HOW TO GROW
A BUSINESS FROM
CONCEPT TO CASH

MICHAEL PARRISH DuDELL

With contributions by

MARK CUBAN, BARBARA CORCORAN, LORI GREINER, ROBRET HERJAVEC, DAYMOND JOHN, and KEVIN O'LEARY

SHARK TANK

TANK

JUMP START

YOUR BUSINESS

KINGSWELL

LOS ANGELES · NEW YORK

Dedicated to all of the trailblazers, creators, doers and innovators—to anyone who's ever been brave enough to try, fail, and try again. This one's for you.

Copyright © 2013 Sony Pictures Television Inc.

All photography © American Broadcasting Companies, Inc.

For information address Kingswell, 1101 Flower Street, Glendale, California 91201.

Library of Congress Cataloging-in-Publication Data

DuDell, Michael Parrish
   Shark tank jump start your business : how to launch and grow a business from concept to cash / Michael Parrish DuDell.
      pages   cm
   ISBN 978-1-4013-1292-3 (pbk.)
   1. New business enterprises.   2. Small business—Management.
3. Strategic planning.   I. Title.
   HD62.5.P377 2013
   658.1'1—dc23
         2013025196

FIRST EDITION

10   9   8   7   6   5

FAC-026988-16070

THIS LABEL APPLIES TO TEXT STOCK

CONTENTS

Foreword by Mark Burnett viii
Introduction 1

PART ONE: TO BE OR NOT TO BE . . . AN ENTREPRENEUR
Catching the Entrepreneurial Fever—Lori Greiner 7
Chapter 1: Small Business 101 9
Chapter 2: What's Your EQ (Entrepreneurial Quotient)? 21
Chapter 3: Your Big Idea 35
Shark Tale: Travis Perry, ChordBuddy (Season 3) 52

PART TWO: SETTING UP SHOP
The Unlikely Entrepreneur—Robert Herjavec 57
Chapter 4: Finding Your Customers 59
Chapter 5: Getting Down to Business 71
Chapter 6: Making It Official 85
Shark Tale: Moshe Weiss, SoundBender (Season 4) 98

PART THREE: MONEY MATTERS
The Art of Success—Kevin O'Leary 103
Chapter 7: Knowing Your Numbers 105
Chapter 8: Understanding Financing 115
Shark Tale: Jim Tselikis and Sabin Lomac,
Cousins Maine Lobster (Season 4) 126

PART FOUR: OPEN FOR BUSINESS
The 100th Road—Daymond John 131
Chapter 9: Up and Running 133
Chapter 10: Mastering Marketing 147
Chapter 11: Learning to Sell 165
Shark Tale: Rick Hopper, ReadeREST (Season 3) 181

PART FIVE: TAKING IT TO THE NEXT LEVEL
The Power of Failure—Barbara Corcoran 187
Chapter 12: You Can't Do It Alone: Building the
Right Team 189
Chapter 13: Leading the Charge 203
Chapter 14: The Smart Way to Grow 217
Shark Tale: Lani Lazzari, Simple Sugars (Season 4) 230

PART SIX: A DIP IN THE TANK: BEHIND-THE-SCENES AT *SHARK TANK*
It Only Takes One—Mark Cuban 235
Chapter 15: Swimming with the Sharks:
A Roundtable Q&A 237
Shark Tale: Tracey Noonan and Danielle Desroches,
Wicked Good Cupcakes (Season 4) 255

Final Words 259

Tools and Resources 261
  My Small Business Jump Start Plan 261
  From Idea to Incorporation: A Flowchart 263
  Talk the Talk: Small Business Terms to Know 265
  Online Resources 268
  Books to Read 274
Notes 277
About the Author 285

FOREWORD BY MARK BURNETT

hark Tank is an important show because it proves the entrepreneurial spirit is alive and well. But even more than that, it gives people hope and inspires future entrepreneurs to pursue their dream of building a business at a time when America needs them the most.

Today, Americans face unprecedented hardships. As the job security they once relied on quickly disappears, people of all ages and backgrounds are reclaiming their future by creating their own opportunities. While this rebirth of small business is exhilarating, it also presents many challenges.

As banks remain wary of giving out loans, *Shark Tank* is stepping up and serving this new crop of entrepreneurs by offering access to six self-made, ultra-successful, millionaire and billionaire business moguls who are looking to invest their own money in the right people with the right ideas.

Each season the Sharks set a new record amount for investments—most recently investing over $10 million. At the same time, each season the entrepreneurs who appear on *Shark Tank* continue to report amazing success stories:

incredible growth, unbelievable sales, and an abundance of job creation within their communities.

It's hard to believe that we went from fewer than two thousand applicants our first season to more than thirty thousand for Season 4. I believe this alone demonstrates that *Shark Tank* inspires not only fledgling *and* seasoned business owners, but also stay-at-home moms and dads with nothing more than an idea. Ultimately, that's why I think the show has been so successful: it strikes a chord with just about anyone who watches it, from successful entrepreneurs to children.

A recent report released by Babson College and Baruch College showed that U.S. entrepreneurship climbed in 2012 to the highest level in a decade. This just years after a crippling recession. I guess in some way we'd like to think that *Shark Tank* has played a small role in the resurgence of entrepreneurism in America. At least we hope it has.

What we do know is that this show gives real people a platform to catapult their dreams and ideas into successful businesses. It proves that with a little ingenuity and a lot of hard work, they can all transform their lives and their communities. That's a powerful message, and one I'm proud to stand behind.

Mark Burnett is an award-winning executive producer who's famous for such hit shows as Shark Tank, The Voice, Survivor, and Celebrity Apprentice.

Burnett has won four Emmy Awards and four People's Choice Awards.

INTRODUCTION

Sure, the walk may only be a few feet, but it feels more like a mile. As you make your way down the dimly lit hallway, two rows of glowing aquariums illuminate the path and guide you toward a pair of large, wooden doors. Although you may not be able to hear the swell of the driving music that underscores your journey, somehow you can still feel it in your body. There's no turning back now. Without even a moment to comprehend what's about to happen, the doors swing open and there you are, standing face-to-face with a panel of world-class investors on national television. You walk front and center, take a deep breath, and begin your pitch. This is the moment. This is the opportunity. This is everything you've been working toward.

As you speak, the Sharks begin furiously scribbling down notes. You can't help but wonder what they're writing, what they're thinking. To them and the rest of the world you're just another eager entrepreneur pitching a new idea, but to you this experience couldn't be more personal. Every day, every month, every year that you've spent tirelessly building your business flashes before your eyes. The moment you first decided to start a company, the day you officially incorporated, your first sale—all of it comes rushing back in a single flash. You try to stay focused, but how can you when each of those thrilling firsts has paved the way to this: the opportunity to land a deal with one of the Sharks.

For the lucky few who enter into the Shark Tank, this is their fate. Whether pitching a food truck, clothing line, or tech company, each fearless entrepreneur takes the same excruciating walk. And yet even though this expedition is a solitary one, somehow you feel as though you're there too, watching from a distance as a small but important piece of history is made. Will the pitch go well? Will a deal be struck? Your guess is as good as anyone's. The only thing you *can* count on is that what you're witnessing is but a tiny snippet in the life of a business—a subchapter of a much larger story that started a long time ago.

The age of entrepreneurship is upon us. In the last three years, the United States has seen the highest rate of new business creation in over a decade, and many of these fledgling companies are being started by first-time entrepreneurs. As technology advances and creates an abundance of new and exciting opportunities, more and more people are mustering up the courage to abandon a career that feels painfully conventional and embrace one that is deeply meaningful.

But it takes more than hunger and desire to achieve success, and with great effort also comes great challenge. The U.S. Small Business Administration reports that more than half of small businesses fail within the first five years—a number that will only continue to rise. And of those businesses that do survive, many struggle to ever achieve significant growth.

So why do entrepreneurs have such a difficult time getting their ventures off the ground? A shortage of capital? A lack of connections? Perhaps. But the modern entrepreneur's greatest barrier is rarely money or community; those are symptoms of a much larger problem. No, the greatest hurdle standing in the way of the first-time small business owner is a general lack of knowledge and know-how—tangible information and experience about how to create, maintain, and grow a company.

There's no question that starting your own business can be a remarkably liberating and fulfilling experience. Each week on *Shark Tank* you witness firsthand how hard work and dedication can turn an eager hopeful into a successful entrepreneur. But just because you *can* start a business doesn't mean that you *should* start a business—or that you'll even enjoy it. Is entrepreneurship the right choice for you? Does your idea have the potential to become a business? This is where *Shark Tank Jump Start Your Business* begins.

In the first part of the book you'll be asked to assess your business idea and evaluate your entrepreneurial skills. The goal is to help you identify, from the start, if you have what it takes to run a profitable company. From there you'll learn how to turn your concept into a business, including everything from incorporation to basic accounting. Next, you'll be guided through the launch process and gain access to crucial knowledge on how to effectively market, sell, and promote your product or service. Finally, you'll discover how to grow your business and achieve long-term success. As an extra bonus, the final part of the book features an exclusive, up-close-and personal round table discussion with all six of the Sharks. But the Sharks' knowledge doesn't end there.

Infused in each chapter are a series of Shark Bites—small bits of wisdom from the Sharks pertaining to each topic. You'll learn what Barbara Corcoran thinks about hiring, why Daymond John believes brand is so valuable, and how Mark

Cuban defines the perfect pitch. You'll discover what Kevin O'Leary looks for in leaders, why Lori Greiner thinks entrepreneurs should protect their ideas, and what Robert Herjavec believes is the secret to closing a sale. What's more, each part of the book will open with an essay by a Shark and close with a behind-the-scenes look at a successful entrepreneur from the show.

Launching a business is an adventure, and begins with that first step. Perhaps this book is that step, or maybe you've already started your business and are looking for new ideas and fresh insights. Whatever your goals may be, *Shark Tank Jump Start Your Business* is the resource you need to take your idea from concept to cash.

The walk down that hallway may only be a few feet, but it feels more like a mile. And it starts right here, right now, with you and your idea. Who knows, perhaps one day you too could be standing in the *Shark Tank*, making a deal that will forever change the course of your life.

PART ONE

TO BE OR NOT TO BE . . . AN ENTREPRENEUR

LORI GREINER

CLAIM TO FAME: Inventor of over 400 products, which have grossed more than $500 million in retail sales, and well-known celebrity personality on QVC-TV.

THE WAY I WORK: "I can tell right away if a product is a zero or a hero. It's just a feeling I get. If it's a hero, I'll invest."

CATCHING THE
ENTREPRENEURIAL FEVER

For me, being an entrepreneur is all about passion and drive. Starting out, I didn't have people who were there to help me and take me by the hand. I had to figure things out on my own, which made me the person I am today. Nobody I knew had ever done anything like what I was attempting, so it really was up to me to figure it out. It made me smarter, I think, and that's really important because the more experienced you are, the stronger, faster, and more responsive you can be—all of which are important qualities for anyone starting out.

Initially, my love of business grew out of a passion for inventing. After my first product did well, the creative juices just started flowing. I couldn't stop. One success led to another, and before I knew it I had the entrepreneurial fever.

As my business began to take off, I grew even more excited about the work. I felt like I was really doing something meaningful—something that made people's lives better. That was very enthralling for me. So I just kept going, inventing more products. That's all I ever thought about.

The entrepreneur will face many challenges along the

way, so you've got to have the discipline and self-motivation to do whatever it takes to get the job done. You have to be willing to do the hard work and put in the long hours. There are times when I've literally worked thirty-six hours straight. [*Author's note:* Case in point, Lori and I are meeting for this interview at 10 P.M. on a Saturday night after she's already put in a full day of filming and travel.]

After launching hundreds of products, my business has become very successful and my entrepreneurial fever has evolved and grown to include other passions as well, like *Shark Tank*.

I absolutely love working on the show because it feels so good to help others achieve the kind of success I've had. The idea of paying it forward is very important to me, and I feel like being on the show has helped me do that. I've always believed that if you're lucky enough to do well, you have a responsibility to give back. That's the higher, truer, bigger meaning of life.

I really do feel as though it's my destiny to be on the show and to serve as a positive role model for other entrepreneurs who are trying to succeed.

1

SMALL BUSINESS 101

I n 1931, the world had just entered a great depression. As the economy tanked and unemployment soared, Americans from California to New York felt the piercing sting of hopelessness and desperation. Following decades of tremendous growth and opportunity, the ebullient spirit that had once defined a nation was now depleted. But somewhere between the unveiling of the Empire State Building and Babe Ruth hitting his six hundredth homerun, a man you've probably never heard of defined an idea that would shape the next century and beyond: the American Dream.

When James Truslow Adams first put those two words together, Americans had yet to adopt prosperity as a core value, let alone a birthright. No matter how inspired Adams may have felt when he first conjured up the idea of the American Dream, he couldn't possibly have known just how transformative those words would become.

As our culture has progressed, the American Dream has matured and evolved. But the heart of the idea has remained as pure as the day it was first declared: the "dream of a land in which life should be better and richer and fuller for everyone, with opportunity for each according to ability or achievement."

Today the entrepreneur has become the very embodiment of that dream. Through hard work and perseverance, it's he or she who dares not only to dream, but to risk everything for the chance to succeed.

When you think of the typical small business, you may imagine your favorite local diner or independent bookstore. Perhaps you picture the kind of quaint mom-and-pop establishment that lines the main streets of cities across America. But *small* business is actually much *bigger* than most people realize. Defined by the Small Business Administration as companies with fewer than five hundred employees, small businesses employ around 60 million people each year, contributing to roughly half of private sector employment. From grocery stores and doctors' offices to consulting firms and advertising agencies, small businesses play a major role in the job market and the economy.

According to a 2009 *USA Today*/Gallup Poll, roughly a quarter of working Americans have considered becoming an entrepreneur. And with more access to resources than ever before, many people are walking away from the safety of their day jobs to do just that. But access should never be mistaken for ease. While a number of rewards come with starting a business, there are an equal number of challenges—challenges that must be considered before launching any new venture.

If you've picked up this book, you have, at the very least, a desire to start your own business. Congratulations, that's the first step. But before you can begin building the next great company, you must first consider a few key questions:

What kind of business do you want to start?

Are you looking to open a small boutique firm or is the goal to create fast and furious growth? Do you want to start a service-based business or is your idea centered on a product? While one type of business isn't necessarily better than another, it's crucial to thoroughly research your industry and market *before* launching a company.

Why are you starting this company?

Perhaps even more significant than the "what" is the "why." Do you want to start a business to avoid working for someone else? Do you have a great idea that you feel would perform well in the market? Are you out of work and looking to gain financial independence? The "why" behind your business will play a major role in many of the decisions you make as an entrepreneur.

Are you willing to invest the time and energy it takes to succeed?

Owning a small business, especially at the beginning, is a 24/7 job. From strategy and development to balancing the books and sweeping the floors, it's likely you'll be a one-man band, at least at the beginning. Don't fool yourself into thinking that you'll start a business next week and sell the company for millions of dollars next year. For most entrepreneurs the road is long and challenging. In fact, a good rule of thumb is to estimate how much time and energy you think you'll need to invest in your new venture and then double that number. Still interested?

What skills or training must you acquire before opening your business?

In Chapter Two you'll be asked to dig deep and identify your strengths and weaknesses, but for now try to anticipate what

"You should never worry about economic timing when starting a new business. When the economy is slow, it means bigger companies are reducing their investments and cutting back, which opens the door to innovation. When the economy is good, companies often rest on their laurels. It's always a good time to start a business in America."

MARK

kind of training or skills you may need to make your company work. If you're great with your hands and would like to open a massage business, there are certain types of certifications you must acquire before you can legally run that type of operation. If you have a great eye for design but not much experience, you may need to develop a few more hard skills before starting a design company. Flesh out your idea and try to anticipate what skills or training you'll need to acquire.

What happens if your business fails?

Optimism is important, especially for the first-time entrepreneur, but so is pragmatism. Since half of all new companies fail within the first five years, you owe it to yourself to consider what might happen if your business faces a similar fate. Will you be financially wiped out or do you have another source of income? Will you be able to get your old day job back or will you face long-term unemployment? While you shouldn't let fear of the unknown deter you from starting a business, you must also not let ignorance lead you down a dangerous path. It's just as important to anticipate failure as it is to prepare for success.

While these types of questions are not easy to ask, their answers will provide tremendous value as you begin to shape your business idea. Launching a business, especially for the first time, is a major undertaking, and preparation is absolutely critical.

MYTHS VS. FACTS

Being an entrepreneur hasn't always been so glamorous. Until the last twenty years or so, the entrepreneur was seen less as an innovator and more as a risk-taker or thrill-seeker. In many circles it was considered foolish and even sometimes careless to launch a new company. Why would you go through the trouble of starting your own organization when there were so many stable corporations to work for? But as technology invigorates the small business landscape and big business stumbles over its own red tape, the playing field is slowly beginning to level.

Still, much misinformation exists about what it takes to be an entrepreneur. Some believe that you must have access to a large amount of capital, while others insist that bootstrapping is the only way to ever succeed. From education and background to economic timing and geographic location, there are a number of confusing and contradictory ideas out there about what it actually takes to start and run a thriving business.

So why exactly do these myths exist? Much of the confusion is fueled by a paralyzing fear of failure. There's comfort in believing there's only one formula for success because it lets you off the hook. It gives you permission to stay at that job you don't like or abandon that "silly idea" you've been dreaming about for years. Never trying is the only way to guarantee you will never fail. But the reality is that the path to success is entirely up to you. Daymond's journey was different from

Barbara's, which was different from Lori's, which was different from Robert's. For every rule there is an exception; for every definite there's a maybe.

To help separate fact from fiction, here's the truth behind a few of the most common small business myths:

Entrepreneurship runs in the family.

While having an entrepreneur in the family can certainly instill some important knowledge and values, the truth is that growing up around entrepreneurs doesn't affect your ability to become one. A study done by the Kauffman Foundation—a renowned organization dedicated to promoting education and entrepreneurship—surveyed 549 company founders across various industries and found that more than half of the participants were first-generation entrepreneurs. In other words, starting a great business isn't about where you came from. It's about where you want to go.

Entrepreneurs are born, not made.

If you can't sing, you'll probably never be a professional singer. Sure, you can take lessons and get better, but if you can't sing, you can't sing. Starting a business is just the opposite: it's a learned skill, not a natural born talent. While it's hard to deny the common traits found in successful entrepreneurs, numerous studies suggest that the majority of small business owners didn't even consider starting a company until much later in life.

You can assess an entrepreneur's potential by how well she performs in college.

While one camp believes that the best entrepreneurs bypass college, the other would argue that college is a breeding ground for excellence. Those assumptions are both true, and false. Yes, some entrepreneurs never attend college and others do exceptionally well. But the majority perform somewhere in the middle. The same Kauffman study from our first example found that 67 percent of the surveyed entrepreneurs ranked their academic performance among the top 30 percent of their undergraduate class. They weren't setting the curve, but they weren't flunking out either. Strangely enough, the study found that high school competency serves as a better indicator than college of future entrepreneurial success.

Not wanting to work for someone else is a good enough reason to start your own company.

Most entrepreneurs don't love the idea of working for somebody else; this is true. But it's rarely the single driving force behind their decision to start a company, and it shouldn't be yours. If it is, you may wish to reconsider your choice. As you'll soon learn, running a business is all-encompassing, and a general dislike for authority may not be enough to keep you going.

Entrepreneurship is a young person's game.

False, false, and false! Another study done by the Kauffman Foundation found that every year from 1996 to 2007, Americans between the ages of fifty-five and sixty-five had a higher rate of entrepreneurial activity than those aged twenty to thirty-four, "averaging a rate of entrepreneurial activity roughly one-third larger than their younger counterparts." Moreover, the study found that the average age of a tech founder is thirty-nine—with "twice as many over 50 as under age 25." By 2011, the number had increased even more, with Americans between the ages of fifty-five and sixty-four making up

20.9 percent of all new entrepreneurs. Think you're too old to start a business? Think again!

Most entrepreneurs are just in it for the money.

If you're starting a business as a way to get rich quick, you may find yourself sorely disappointed. On average, small business owners actually make substantially *less* money than they would working for someone else. What's more, they typically put in more hours, deal with more stress, and have more responsibilities. As Lori Greiner often says, "Entrepreneurs are the only people who will work eighty hours a week to avoid working forty." If making a quick buck is your only motivation, you may be in for a long, frustrating journey.

You must be wealthy or have access to a lot of capital to start a business.

You may need a lot of energy and stamina to launch a company, but you don't always need a lot of money. It's estimated that the average startup cost for a business is somewhere between $25,000 and $50,000, depending on whether or not the company plans to hire employees. And where do most entrepreneurs get that money? Not from a bank, not from their family. Most business owners use money from their personal savings to start their company. In fact, studies suggest that around 65 percent of entrepreneurs finance their venture using some form of personal debt.

You shouldn't start a business during a recession.

What do Burger King, GE, Microsoft, and Hyatt Hotels all have in common? They were all started during a recession. While you may think that starting a business during a recession is a bad idea, many companies have thrived during difficult economic times. It actually makes a lot sense if you think about it. During a recession you may have better access to cheaper space and more talented employees. And because everyone is trying to save money, you may have a greater shot at competing than you would in a time of prosperity. Hopefully, by the time the market recovers, you'll have already gone through the difficult startup phase and be on your way to growing the business.

Now that you know some of the myths, here's the truth: starting a business is simultaneously one of the most rewarding and difficult things you could ever do. There will be moments, plenty of them in fact, of uncertainty and fear. After your second month of working seven days a week or your second year without a regular paycheck, you'll begin to seriously question why you were ever crazy enough to start a company in the first place. But when that moment occurs, and eventually it will, you can't let it get in your way. Instead, you must use that anxiety as a catapult to push you to the next level.

When you decide to become an entrepreneur, you enter into an exclusive club with members like Steve Jobs, Thomas Edison, and Warren Buffett. You may never receive a tote bag or newsletter, but make no mistake: you will earn that membership each and every day. And if that club had an oath, it would

SHARK BITE

"One of the biggest myths is that it costs a lot of money to start a business. Venture capital may get all the sexy media attention, but most small businesses are started on a bootstrap budget. Most people will have an opportunity to start a million-dollar business— not a billion-dollar one. And you don't need a lot of money in today's economy to start that."

ROBERT

SHARING THE SPOTLIGHT: A WORD ON PARTNERSHIPS

Starting a company on your own can feel overwhelming, especially for the first-time small business owner. With a seemingly endless to-do list, it can feel as though your job is never done. So for many, the idea of working with a partner can be very appealing. More people on board equals less responsibility and ultimately less headache, right? Not always. Bringing on a cofounder is a huge decision that will have a major impact on your business. Whether that impact is positive or negative is up to you.

As in any relationship, the secret to a great partnership is communication and trust. Remember, you're not just hiring an employee; this person will have access to every facet of the business. Therefore, it's crucial that you're able to have open and honest conversations with your partner about anything and everything related to the business.

It's also important to look for someone with a different set of skills and talents than your own. If you're exceptional at sales and marketing, for instance, you should seek out a partner who is great at accounting or strategy. If you're a left-brained, analytical thinker, you may wish to find a more right-brained, big-picture type of person. You want to create a well-rounded team.

Although it's natural to consider friends and family members as prospective partners, that may not always be the wisest choice. No matter how much you like someone or how well you get along, conflict is bound to occur—guaranteed! If you decide to start a company with a friend or family member, make sure you've discussed how you'll seperate your personal and professional lives.

Regardless of whom you partner with, you'll want to put together a comprehensive partnership agreement. From financial expectations to roles and responsibilities, this document protects both founders and should lay out all the nitty-gritty details of your working relationship. You never know what conflicts lie ahead.

Companies like Microsoft and Google, have proven that there can be power in numbers, but bringing on a partner isn't the right move for every business owner. Make sure it's the best choice for you and your company before asking someone to come on board.

2

WHAT'S YOUR EQ (ENTREPRENEURIAL QUOTIENT)?

It's estimated that each day some 2,356 Americans become entrepreneurs. From college students and stay-at-home moms to seniors and ex–corporate executives, together these scrappy, homegrown pioneers will open more than 500,000 businesses annually in hopes of building the next great company.

So, which companies will thrive and which will fail? Only time will tell. But perhaps there's a more productive question. Maybe the real indicator lies not in the business but in the business *owner*. Are some more fit to be entrepreneurs than others? Is there a type of person who has a better shot at building a successful company than someone else? While there are no scientific answers to these questions, many experts would agree that there is a very well-defined entrepreneurial mind-set.

Below you'll find a short test that's designed to help determine if *you* have the right combination of skills, talents, and instincts to become an entrepreneur. Read each statement below and respond with either "yes," "sometimes," or "no." From there, assign each answer a corresponding point and tally up your numbers to reveal your score.

WHAT'S YOUR EQ?

KEY
YES: TWO POINTS
SOMETIMES: ONE POINT
NO: ZERO POINTS

1   I'm driven by achievement and success. _____
2   When I experience failure, I'm quick to bounce back. _____
3   I consider myself to be self-motivated and self-sufficient. _____
4   I have been told I'm a natural salesperson. _____
5   I don't like the idea of working for somebody else. _____
6   I'm great at thinking on my feet. _____
7   I have superior communication abilities. _____
8   I run towards challenges instead of backing
     away from them. _____
9   I have a strong opinion—sometimes too strong. _____
10 I consider myself a leader. _____
11 I like doing things my own way and question
     conventional wisdom. _____
12 I hold myself to a higher standard. _____
13 I work as hard or harder than anyone else I know. _____
14 I have friends or family members who run their
     own business. _____
15 I'm great at making decisions, even if I don't always
     make the right one. _____
16 People think of me as intense or passionate. _____
17 I'm more risk-seeking than risk-averse. _____
18 I enjoy coming up with new ideas. _____
19 I don't know how, but things usually seem to work
     out for me. _____
20 When I set my mind to something, I see it through. _____

TOTAL: _____

RESULTS

40–31 points: Good news! It looks like you were born to be an entrepreneur. With the perfect combination of passion, drive, and fortitude, you have exactly what it takes to run a business. In fact, it's surprising you've lasted this long working for somebody else.

30–21 points: You certainly have the potential to be a great entrepreneur, but you may face some challenges along the way. Perhaps you take pleasure in working for someone else or avoid challenges. Maybe you have a difficult time finishing what you've started or tend to be overly risk-averse. Whatever your personal barriers may be, take note of them as you begin your journey.

20 and under: Even though you may have the desire to start a company, it's likely your experience will be fraught with challenges. Rememeber, you don't have to be an entrepreneur to be entrepreneurial. There are plenty of opportunities to exercise your independent nature within already established companies. You may wish to think twice about whether starting a business is really the right move for you.

So how did you do? Are you destined to become an entrepreneur, or should you consider exploring other opportunities?

Keep in mind that this test is designed to educate, not discourage. While a clearly defined mind-set does exist, there are plenty of talented entrepreneurs who have broken the mold.

SHARK BITE

"Great entrepreneurs definitely have a certain nature about them. That's been proven. Typically they are type A; they're very driven; they're risk-takers. I'm not saying you have to be that way to make it, but I certainly feel as though most entrepreneurs have a very specific type of personality."

LORI

With enough drive and determination, most anyone can start a company—and that means you too.

IDENTIFYING STRENGTHS AND WEAKNESSES

No matter how you scored on the EQ test, you should be aware of your personal strengths and weaknesses from the start. Identifying this information will help you make essential decisions about whom to work with, how to structure your position, and even what kind of business to build. While some people excel at this type of exercise, others may find it exceedingly difficult.

This process is valuable because it determines where you should direct your efforts. Professional achievement relies less on your aptitude for developing new skills than on your ability to fine-tune the ones you already have.

Making this type of assessment can feel overwhelming. So, to help focus the process, try to think of it in the context of starting a new business. Which parts excite you? Which parts are you dreading?

Below you'll find a breakdown of the five essential phases every entrepreneur goes through when starting a new business. Use these categories to help identify your primary strengths and weaknesses. The sooner you can name them, the more productive you'll be.

Brainstorming: A great business starts with a great concept. Are you bursting at the seams with new ideas or do you struggle with generating them? Do you prefer brainstorming with a team or do you work better alone? Where in the ideation process do you excel and where do you stall? For some people, coming up with the idea is the easiest part. Others approach this process with anxiety and fear. What strengths and weaknesses does the process bring out in you?

Strategy: Having an idea is great, but having a plan is crucial. How strategic are you? Would you say you're more of a dreamer or a planner? Are you consistently five steps ahead or do you prefer staying grounded and in the moment? Being an entrepreneur requires a certain amount of strategic thinking, and some people are naturally better at that than others. Where do you fall on the spectrum?

Organization: Organization is important to all businesses, but not to all entrepreneurs. Would you call yourself detail-oriented? Do you do great with deadlines? Are you motivated by order, process, and procedure? It's all right if organization isn't your strong suit, but come to grips with it now, so you can prepare accordingly and bring on the right support team.

Communication: You can have the greatest business in the world, but if you can't communicate your product or service, you'll never succeed. Are you a natural born salesperson? Do you love to connect with customers and employees? Do you do your best work when speaking, writing, or expressing yourself? Getting your message across is vital to the overall well-being of your business. How strong a communicator are you?

Execution: A plan is essential, but only if it's properly executed. Do you get excited about the creative process but lose focus when it's time to execute? Would you rather dream up a project than actually launch it? Do you value process over performance? Eventually your business will reach a point where its very livelihood will rely on the precision of your execution. Do you have the right combination of skills to make it work?

Of course you will have more strengths and weaknesses

SHARK BITE

"*People believe you need to be a well-rounded person and work on your weaknesses. That's just not true. To compete on a world-class level, you need to accentuate your strengths. Focus on the things you're good at and hire someone to do the rest.*"

ROBERT

than just what may fall under these five categories. But hopefully through this process you've begun to uncover some common themes. Take a few moments to make your own comprehensive list. It's important to be honest here. If you're not great at execution but wish you were, you should still count it as a weakness. You can work on improving your skill sets later. For now, the goal is to simply assess your current state.

Once you have developed a list of your strengths and weaknesses, begin taking note of where you should spend your time and what responsibilities you should outsource. If strategy or organization is not your strong suit, you may want to think about bringing on an associate or administrator. If you're not great at execution or ideation, perhaps you should find a business partner who is. Identifying your strengths and weaknesses is a simple exercise that can have a dramatic impact on your business.

GETTING EDUCATED: TRADITIONAL VS. DIY

If you interview a group of prosperous entrepreneurs, it's likely you'll uncover some interesting similarities, many of which were represented in the EQ test you took earlier in the chapter. But no matter how many common traits you might find, there's one area that's almost always diverse: educational background.

For many years, most people who wanted to work in the business sector pursued a more traditional path. Success, many believed, could be achieved by following a time-tested formula. Those days are long gone.

Survey a group of successful business owners today, and you'll quickly see just how varied educational backgrounds can be. While some choose to take a more traditional route, perhaps even earning an MBA, others drop out of high school to start their first company or transition from another field altogether. In the modern, globalized world, business success has become more about pluck and ingenuity than grades and formalities, especially for the entrepreneur.

For many, the issue of higher education comes down to money. Depending on which school you choose to attend, the price tag for an MBA can range from thousands to hundreds of thousands of dollars. With a tepid job market and a fickle economy, it's very possible to spend $150,000 on a graduate-level education only to find yourself out of work and in serious debt. As the cost of a starting a company decreases, the price of traditional education becomes harder to justify.

"I am a huge believer that you go to college to learn how to learn," writes Mark Cuban on his blog. "However, if that goal is subverted because traditional universities, public and private, charge so much to make that happen, I believe that system will collapse and there will be better alternatives created."

Many business hopefuls share Mark's point of view and are hungrily searching for alternative options. Some are even creating their own educational opportunities. With more access to information, media, and community online, creating a DIY path can save the entrepreneur precious time and money.

But choosing that route requires a tremendous amount of dedication and discipline.

Below you'll find five ways to help kick-start the learning process. Even if you choose to seek a more traditional education, these tips will come in handy.

Read everything: No experience in accounting? Unsure of how to build a marketing campaign? While this book is a fantastic start, it should be just that—a start. Commit to reading a minimum of two business books by trusted experts each month. You should also begin subscribing to business-related magazines, like *Fast Company*, *INC.*, and *Entrepreneur*. Publications like these provide a real-time snapshot of what's happening in the small business community—a valuable resource for anyone interested in becoming an entrepreneur. For more of this type of material, including a list of recommended books by established business voices, check out the Tools and Resources section at the end of this book.

Explore digital tools: Getting in the habit of reading new material every day is important, but your research shouldn't stop there. From videos to online courses, the Internet is full of incredible tools for the blossoming entrepreneur. In fact, the greatest challenge is the abundance of material, not the lack thereof. To help focus your search, start following some of your favorite business authors and publications on Twitter and Facebook. Take note of what they're recommending on a daily basis. Try to commit an hour or two each day to finding valuable digital content. Download apps that can help boost your productivity. Sign up for newsletters. Listen to business podcasts. While the exploration process can feel daunting at first, over time you'll begin to see just how much this information can help you grow.

Invest in community: The value of community cannot be overstated, especially when trying to launch a new business. If you're comfortable with social media, dive right in and join the conversation. Most entrepreneurs are nothing if not boisterous and outspoken; you'll have no trouble finding these rabble-rousers online. But don't spend all your time in front of a screen. You should also seek out offline community as well. Explore local meetups and small business associations, attend trade shows and conferences, and reach out to other entrepreneurs in your field. If you live in a major metropolitan area, you may find it helpful to join a co-working space—a shared working environment that houses a variety of companies. If you're going to create your own educational experience, you must be even more proactive when it comes to building community.

Get some experience: Most entrepreneurs need all the help they can get. Try to find a small startup that interests you and see if you can spend a few hours each week helping out. It's possible they won't be able to pay you, but don't let that be a deterrent. Think of it as an internship. If you can't find an opportunity, launch something small on your own—a starter business. If you're crafty, sell something on Etsy. If you have stuff in your house to get rid of, create your own eBay store. Start something small that requires a minimal investment. This will help prepare you for what it's like to run a larger operation. Experience is the greatest teacher of them all.

Find a mentor: We live in a culture that places tremendous value on independence and self-reliance. But knowing how and when to ask for help, especially when it's hard, is one of the most valuable lessons you can learn. A great mentor can play an influential role in your personal life and the life of

"Technology has really changed education by allowing more people to get information quicker than ever before. It's no longer necessary to always take that two-, four-, or eight-year course. You can learn so much on your own."

DAYMOND

your business. Seek out a relationship with someone in your community whom you respect and trust.

Whether you get an MBA or decide to build your own curriculum, be sure your path includes the right combination of knowledge, experience, and connection. A well-rounded education requires all three of these priceless elements.

GETTING YOUR LIFE(STYLE) IN ORDER

The final piece of the puzzle in deciding whether entrepreneurship is the right fit for you is assessing the current state of your personal and professional life. In other words, before you can get your *business* in order, you must get your *life* in order. But what exactly does that mean? How do you possibly prepare for the unknown? It starts by examining three key areas:

Time: Did you just undertake a massive new project at your day job? Do you have a plethora of outside commitments that limit your downtime? If you want your company to succeed, it must be your primary focus for the first few months, if not years. Every free minute should be spent building and growing the business. This isn't to imply that you should ditch all your other responsibilities; it just means that your company must remain front and center.

If you generally have a hectic schedule, you may find it helpful to schedule "business-building" time in your calendar, as you would a meeting. And don't just pencil it in; literally schedule nonnegotiable "business development" hours. If you find yourself with less than ten hours a week to dedicate to your business, you should probably hold off until your schedule is a bit more flexible. Time is your most valuable resource, and your new business will demand the majority of it.

Finances: As you'll soon learn, starting a business may require a sizeable personal investment. If you've decided to quit your job or aren't currently working, you must be even more careful with your money. Try to get your overhead—such as rent—as low as possible and reduce your discretionary spending as much as you can. There's no reason to sugarcoat it: the first couple years will likely be very financially challenging. Be realistic with yourself about whether or not you're really in financial shape to start a business.

Relationships: Starting a new business is like riding a roller coaster, with ups and downs coming toward you at the speed of light. Having a strong support system can significantly reduce the anxiety and stress you're bound to encounter. But it's even more important to pay close attention to your weak

ROBERT

SHARK BITE

"The reality is that when you're starting a business, you have one master to serve—and that's your business. There is no balance. And you have to be honest with yourself. If you're not prepared to make that sacrifice and commitment, don't do it."

VICTORIES, BIG AND SMALL: SETTING SMART GOALS

Regular, strategic goal setting is one of the best habits you can adopt as an entrepreneur. When you start setting goals, the mystery behind success begins to disappear.

As Daymond John says, "Goal setting is like a motto, a hook, or a phrase that's always on your mind, just like a jingle you'd remember from a commercial. The things you do, say, or hear in your everyday life will subconsciously trigger you to act out your goals and move closer to the desired target. A lot of work and thought processes go into goal setting, but once you get the hang of it, it will come to you naturally."

When setting goals, you may find it helpful to use the SMART method, which was first developed by author George T. Doran in 1981. Using this method, goals should meet the following criteria:

Specific: Who? What? Where? When? Why? In order to create truly achievable goals, you must learn to get as specific as possible. If you desire wealth, for instance, your goal shouldn't be to get rich but to make a specific amount of money in a certain period of time.

Measurable: If you can't measure it, you'll never be able to achieve it. When setting goals, it's best to identify short- and long-term measurements of success along the way. This way, you can track your progress in real time.

Attainable: There's nothing wrong with dreaming big, but make sure your goals are somewhat attainable. If you want a million dollars and you only have $100 in your bank account, it's highly unlikely that you'll be a millionaire by next month.

Relevant: Achieving any major goal takes a lot of work, so you must make sure your goals are relevant and important. Don't forget to zoom out a bit and take a look at the bigger picture. Do your short-term goals set you up for long-term success?

Timely: Goals can only become accomplishments when given a target date. Be sure to assign each of your goals a specific due date, and don't allow yourself the opportunity to waver. A time frame will help create a sense of urgency around the goal and push you that much farther ahead.

Write down some of your short- and long-term goals and begin assessing them using the SMART method. Are you right on track, or do some of your goals need a little fine-tuning?

3

YOUR BIG IDEA

Business owners can be called a lot of things: job creators, entrepreneurs, founders. But no matter the title, they all share one single, underlying goal: the desire to solve a problem. Whether you're inventing something new or simply developing a new approach, a great business starts with a great solution. You need only look at a handful of companies featured on *Shark Tank* to see this principle in practice:

SURFSET Fitness, Season 4, Deal made with Mark Cuban

SURFSET Fitness, Season 4, deal made with Mark Cuban

Problem: Surfing is a fantastic total-body workout, but not everyone has time for it or access to the beach.

Solution: SURFSET Fitness workouts allow anyone to get the benefits of surfing by using a free standing SURFSET Fitness board designed to mimic the movement of its aquatic counterpart.

Cozy Bug, Season 4, Deal made with Daymond John

Cozy Bug, Season 4, deal with Daymond John

Problem: Kids outgrow clothes quickly, which can end up costing parents an arm and a leg.

Solution: Cozy Bug products are designed to grow with the child, allowing clothes to be worn for many years and saving parents time and money.

Scrub Daddy, Season 4, Deal with Lori Greiner

Problem: Cleaning a variety of products often requires the use of more than one tool.

Solution: The Scrub Daddy sponge uses a special foam that changes texture in different temperatures of water, allowing it to serve as the perfect cleaning instrument for any task.

So as you can see, a great business starts with a great solution. Below you'll find ten questions designed to help effectively evaluate your idea. If answered thoroughly, these questions should provide the clarity you'll need to advance to the next stage of building your business.

What problem are you trying to solve, and how will you solve it?

Don't think too hard here. Simply identify the problem and briefly explain the solution your business will offer.

Is someone else already solving this problem?

Most likely there are other people trying to solve the same problem that you are. That's not necessarily a bad thing. Watch closely and study each part of their business. You might discover that by making only a small tweak you can capture a large piece of the market.

How is your solution better and/or different than your competitors'?

Assuming you will in fact have some competition, you must next identify how you'll differentiate your product or service from others. What are you bringing to the table that's different and/or better than what's already out there?

Is there a want or need for the product or service?

Maybe you've come up with a brilliant new way to teach corporate executives how to whistle. Great! But do enough people want or need that? Probably not. Before you go through the trouble of starting a company, you must first uncover whether there's a genuine desire for it in the marketplace.

How big is the potential market?

Although there must be a market for your business, it doesn't have to be huge to achieve results. Plenty of companies do well by targeting very small, niche consumer segments. To discover the size of your market, first gather data on how many people already use your product or service—you can easily find this type of information online. If you're selling dog food, for instance, do research on how many dog owners exist in the U.S. Next, you'll want to eliminate consumers who don't apply to your business. If your dog food is especially designed for small dogs, all pet owners with large canines are out. Finally, try to estimate how much of the market you can capture based on your size and marketing abilities. This last step is the toughest because it's the most subjective. You may find it helpful to look at annual sales of your competitors. How much of the market do they already own?

How much will it cost to start the business?

This may be a tough question to answer at this point in the process, but it's still good to consider. If you're planning to open a retail store, for example, you'll need significantly more capital than you would to start a consulting business. Think hard about the costs associated with launching your business and start tallying up the numbers.

How soon can you start the business?

Does your business require permits and licenses that take months to secure? Do you need to raise substantial capital before you even begin? Developing a solid time frame will provide the perspective you need to make bigger decisions later.

What personal and professional adjustments must you make to start this business?

Most likely, you'll start building your business on nights and weekends while you work toward proof of concept. But even that requires certain personal and professional adjustments. Think about any changes you may need to make to be more successful.

What is (are) your ultimate goal(s) in starting this business?

Do you want to make millions of dollars or build a small, modestly sized family business? Are you looking to sell your company quickly or do you want to create a business that can last a lifetime? The best way to fast-track success is to declare it from the start.

What will happen if you don't start this business?

What if you walk away right now and don't pursue this idea? What will happen, or not happen, in your life and the lives of others if you close this book and go back to what you were doing before? This powerful question can sometimes be the defining factor for an entrepreneur.

But is starting a business really all about solving a problem? What about passion? Shouldn't it play a role in what kind of company you choose to start? That's a complicated question. Being passionate about your work is important, and you certainly must love your product or service. But there's a major difference between being passionate about your business and starting a business based on a passion.

Passions shift over time, and building a company around something so fleeting can be unwise. What's more, passions don't always translate into businesses—both operationally or financially. Loving art and owning an art gallery, for instance, are two very different things. Likewise, taking pleasure in reg-

SHARK BITE

"There are really only two questions to ask when evaluating your business idea: Is there a real need for the product and are enough people willing to pay for it? And if it's been done a million times before, you also have to ask whether you really have a point of difference that makes it so much better. You should never be afraid to fully examine your idea, even if it means you might have to give it up."

BARBARA

ularly cooking for friends and family doesn't mean you'll experience that same joy if you own a restaurant. Passion is only a single ingredient; it's not the recipe.

When it comes to following a passion, you may find it helpful to heed Mark Cuban's advice. Cuban believes the key is to follow your effort, not your passion. "Time is the most valuable asset you don't own," says Cuban. And "how you use or don't use your time is going to be the best indication of where your future is going to take you."

DEVELOPING A PRODUCT

Now that you've evaluated your business idea, you've probably found yourself in one of two positions: (1) you're even more confident in your idea than before and ready to move forward, or (2) you've decided your initial concept is not the strongest choice, and you've begun to rethink the plan.

If it's the former, and your business is centered on a product, the next step is to think about development. In other words, how will you turn your concept into an actual product?

The first step is to hire a professional designer or engineer. Even if you have a sketch of what you'd like the product to look like, you'll still need someone to create a CAD (computer-aided design) file, which is required to make a prototype.

For Travis Perry, founder of ChordBuddy, his search started on Google.

"I had a concept drawing, but I needed to get it designed by a professional," recounts Perry. "So I began Googling 'engineers who play the guitar' and ended up finding an engineer who had a son that played the guitar. He loved the idea and really understood the vision."

Once the engineer designs your product and creates the

CAD file, you'll need to find a company that can create an actual prototype.

When it comes to getting a prototype produced, there are a variety of different options to consider. Perry chose to build an SLA (stereolithography) prototype, which is essentially a type of 3-D printing. Even as one of the more affordable options, it ended up costing somewhere between $750 and $1,000. That may not sound like a lot, but consider that Travis went through seventeen different prototypes before he was ready to get a mold produced.

"A mold is not what I thought it was," says Perry. "Mine was the size of a refrigerator and cost about $150,000 to build."

Finally, when the mold has been tweaked to perfection, the final step is to design and produce the packaging.

Although this entire process can be taxing and expensive, the result is a consumer-ready product.

TANK TIP

"Take advantage of all the resources you can. I didn't know a lot about running a business when I first started, but thanks to SCORE (the Service Core of Retired Executives) I was able to get some really amazing free help. Resources like that can make a huge difference."

—TRACEY NOONAN, COFOUNDER OF WICKED GOOD CUPCAKES

BUYING A BUSINESS

If starting your own company doesn't appeal to you, there are still other ways to be a small business owner. Many choose to purchase a company that's already up and running.

Depending on your particular circumstance, purchasing a business, as opposed to starting one from scratch, can actually be the better option. For one, there's generally less risk involved in buying a business. Think about it: if you purchase a business for $100,000 that has an annual cash flow of $20,000, there's a high probability that you'll recoup your initial investment and begin making a profit in a reasonable time frame. And that's without making any improvements.

Even if you only spend a third of that capital to launch a startup, the likelihood of it being lucrative from the start is slim. Many entrepreneurs are unable to take a salary for the first few years. And for those that do, the size of that salary is less impressive than you might think. It's estimated that a small business owner with less than one year of experience will earn as little as $34,000 a year. By purchasing a business that's already making money, you greatly decrease your overall risk of failure.

Another benefit of buying a business is that you acquire basic infrastructure. A business that's already operational comes with customers, employees, best practices, technology, and other necessities that could take years to develop from the ground up. Add that to the brand loyalty and legacy you'll inherit, and you have the makings of what could be a fantastic business. If you purchase the right company, your main focus will be on improvement, not development. That alone can save you an abundance of time, money, and headache.

Purchasing a business, however, isn't as easy as it may sound. Although you may not be starting something from scratch, you should invest the same level of care and consideration in the evaluation process. When looking to buy a potential business, here are six questions to consider:

Is there potential for growth?

If you're going through the complicated and risky process of purchasing a company, you want to make sure it has real growth potential. Explore not only the business, but the industry as well. Try to identify any market trends that indicate where your business may be headed. ACTION ITEM: Do a comprehensive online search for any information related to the industry. Read articles, find experts, follow fellow entrepreneurs on Twitter.

What are the business's greatest strengths and weaknesses?

You probably have a good idea of the company's strengths. Why else would you be considering buying it? But having a clear understanding of its biggest weaknesses is sometimes even more valuable. As the new owner, you will be the one responsible not only for recognizing the challenges that lie ahead, but for coming up with solutions as well. ACTION ITEM: Anonymously chat with the competition about the business or ask to speak directly with current customers. Don't hold back when having these conversations. You want the most accurate feedback possible.

What kind of reputation does the business have?

There's more to a business than just its current (and potential) financial state. What kind of reputation does it have? What role does it play in the community? Make sure there aren't any unpleasant surprises that could affect your ability to succeed. ACTION ITEM: Review sites like Yelp that give access to real customer feedback. If possible, chat with current and past employees to get their take on the business you're thinking of purchasing.

Why is the business being sold?

Maybe the company is growing too fast for the current owner to handle. Perhaps the founder is ready to retire. Whatever the reason, you'll want to know exactly why the company is being sold. Be sure to ask this question a few times throughout the process and make sure the story holds up. The more information you can gather, the better off you'll be. ACTION ITEM: Don't just talk to management; try to engage the staff as well. If you're thinking about purchasing a retail business, it may also be a good idea to chat with the business's neighbors. Word travels fast, and they may know more than you think.

What does the competition look like?

Even if this information is laid out in the business plan, be sure to have a detailed conversation (or two) with the current owner about the competitive landscape. Who are the company's main competitors? Where are they located? How long have they been around? Look beyond the current competition and explore any potential future challenges as well. If a big competitor is slated to come to town in the near future, for instance, you may be less inclined to purchase the business. ACTION ITEM: Acting as a customer, anonymously reach out to any major competitors and inquire if they're planning to open a new location near you anytime soon.

Will you be able to add value?

This is perhaps the most crucial question of them all. Are you the best person to own this business? Do you have the right combination of skills and talents to maintain and grow the operation? Even if the company seems poised for greatness, you should only purchase a business if you feel certain you can add considerable value to the operation. Answering this question honestly from the start will save you tremendous pain and anguish later. ACTION ITEM: Thoroughly review the list of strengths and weaknesses you created in the

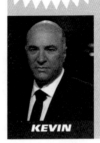

"When you start a business from scratch you have to go through the genesis of trials and tribulations that come with launching a new company. Ultimately, that's what makes good entrepreneurs into great ones. When you buy a business that's already up and running, you miss out on that opportunity."

KEVIN

previous chapter and make sure they align with your role in the business.

Purchasing a business is a complicated process, and you'll eventually need to hire a team to perform the proper due diligence. This begins when the buyer and seller sign a letter of intent. From there, the potential buyer has sixty to ninety days to uncover any unsavory information that may be lurking in the background. The due diligence process usually contains three parts—operational, financial, and legal—and should be performed by a lawyer and accountant who specialize in the process. You'll want to hire the very best team you can afford. This is not the place to cut corners.

Although buying a business can have less financial risk in the long term, it generally requires substantial capital at the start. While banks are usually more inclined to give loans to businesses with cash flow, more than likely you'll be taking on a significant debt. Make sure you have all the necessary information before making such a hefty commitment.

PURCHASING A FRANCHISE

If you'd rather not take on the risk of starting a new business and you're uninterested or unable to purchase one, opening a franchise may be the right decision for you. A franchise is "a business system in which private entrepreneurs purchase the rights to open and run a location of a larger company." Think about a local fast-food restaurant, gym, or hotel chain. It's likely all of those are franchises.

When purchasing a franchise, the business owner (also know as the franchisee) signs a contract with the parent company, in which he agrees to an elaborate set of rules and procedures that must be followed. While some may take pleasure in such a rigid structure, many entrepreneurs hate the idea of being kept on a tight leash.

Before deciding whether purchasing a franchise is the right move, you should know the pros and cons that come with owning this type of business.

Business model

Pro: You're not only buying the business, you're buying the business model as well. For many startups, finding a viable business model can be challenging. By tapping into a proven model, you could have a better chance of success.

Con: Having to follow a specific model limits your ability to control your business. If you come up with a fantastic new idea that's outside the boundaries of the particular model, you may not be allowed to see it through.

Inventory

Pro: In theory, the collective bargaining power of the parent company allows the franchisee to save money on inventory.

Con: The less control you have over inventory, the less control you have over your finances. There's often speculation that franchisors receive kickbacks from suppliers, which means you may become subject to inflated prices.

Startup costs

Pro: When a franchise is being purchased, the parent company will generally provide the franchisee with a good estimation of the startup costs. This allows you to budget properly from the start.

Con: Along with the regular expenses incurred when starting a new business, most franchisors require a nonrefundable initial startup fee that can range from thousands to hundreds of thousands of dollars. This can put the business deep in debt before it even opens.

Cash flow

Pro: When business owners tap into a turnkey operation, one that requires little to no additional work from the buyer, it's assumed that they will begin bringing in cash relatively quickly.

Con: Many franchisors take royalty fees each month, along with requiring business owners to contribute to an advertising fund—even if the advertising doesn't directly affect their particular franchise. Moreover, some franchisors require credit card processing to be done through their system, meaning the franchisee must wait longer than usual to receive her money. Regular expenses like this can dramatically hurt a franchisee's cash flow.

Brand

Pro: An established brand can increase a company's ability to stand out from the competition and acquire new customers, making the business more profitable.

Con: When the parent company does something unfavorable, it has the potential to affect the franchise too. Take BP, for instance, whose Gulf oil spill significantly affected their franchisees' business.

SHARK BITE

"Starting from zero is the hardest thing to do. It's very difficult to start from nothing and create something. Anytime something is more established, you're going to be better off. So a franchise is a great way to start a business because you're working within the confines of somebody else's vision, which of course has its negatives too."

ROBERT

Owning a franchise requires a lot of work, but it's definitely the most "plug and play" option for starting a business. Keep in mind, however, that it may not be the best fit for a person who craves freedom. If the franchisee steps just a little out of bounds, it can cause the parent company to terminate the agreement on a moment's notice. And since most franchisees are forced to sign away the ability to seek legal recourse, the business owner could be out his entire investment.

While this book is designed to help all entrepreneurs jump start their respective businesses, it's important to note that some of the information found in these pages may not be applicable to franchise owners. Most franchises come with stringent operating agreements that affect everything from accounting and marketing to suppliers and customer acquisition. You may find that your franchise contract goes against some of the advice provided in this book. If so, void this information and follow the rules laid out in your agreement. Otherwise, you may not have a business at all.

CHANGING COURSE: UNDERSTANDING THE PIVOT

In 2008, tech entrepreneur Eric Ries introduced an idea called the "Lean Startup" which greatly impacted the startup world. Ries's Lean Startup relies on a constant state of building, measuring, and learning to create the very best product possible. Not only did this approach change the way products are made, but it introduced a slew of new concepts into the business vernacular, including one of today's hottest buzzwords: "pivot."

According to Ries, pivoting is "a structured course correction designed to test a new fundamental hypothesis about the product, strategy, and engine of growth." Put more simply, it's a way of describing startups that change direction but still remain rooted in their original idea. When a business pivots, the vision might change, but the defining principles stay relatively the same.

You most often see pivoting in tech startups, as they have the most data at their disposal. One such example was 3degrees—an app that used Facebook to help people make new offline connections. The idea was simple, users logged in with Facebook and could search their friends' friends for shared interests like "rock climbing," "salsa dancing," or "entrepreneurship." From there, they could reach out directly to the new contact or get an introduction from the mutual friend.

Shortly after launching the app, founder Brian Scordato noticed something interesting: No one wanted to go rock climbing. No one wanted to go salsa dancing. All anyone was doing was searching for their friends' single friends. Even though 3degrees had already gotten some good press, Scordato knew that if he wanted the business to be successful, he had to pivot. A few months later, 3degrees turned into Find Your Lobster—a socially integrated mobile dating app that helps people find their friends' single friends.

"It took months of research before I felt comfortable

pivoting," says Scordato. "Just because the metrics were telling me to build a dating site didn't mean I could build a successful one. I didn't want to waste my time or energy, and only proceeded once I'd done serious diligence."

In this chapter you were asked to evaluate your idea, but the learning shouldn't stop there. The modern entrepreneur must learn to continually improve her product. As you prepare to launch, create checkpoints along the way to reassess and reevaluate key areas of your business. You never know, one day you may need to pivot yourself.

TRAVIS PERRY, CHORDBUDDY (SEASON 3)

BIG IDEA: A device that helps novice guitar players learn to play chords
INVESTOR: Robert Herjavec

Since Travis Perry can remember, he's been crazy about the guitar. Learning to play at only eight years old, he knew from an early age that music would forever be a staple in his life. In 1980, at just eighteen years old, Travis got his first job, teaching guitar at a small music shop in Dothan, Alabama. But after only a few months, he offered his resignation.

"I went to the owner and told him I had to quit," says Travis. "I thought I must have really stunk as a guitar teacher, because half of my students were quitting."

To Travis's surprise, the owner revealed that on average 70 percent of students give up during the first six to eight weeks. In fact, it even has a name: the two-month hump. Travis's dropout rate wasn't bad at all; it was outstanding. "I knew then that our system of teaching guitar was broken."

Determined to create a solution, Travis came up with the idea for ChordBuddy, a small device that fits on the neck of a guitar and helps the novice musician make chords.

"This way, you can get the rhythms down," says Travis. "That's where the music is."

But Travis's idea remained only an idea, and he eventually moved to Nashville to pursue his dream of becoming a professional musician.

Thirty years later, after a rewarding career in the music industry, Travis Perry returned to his home state of Alabama to start a real estate business. But when the industry tanked, so too did his company. The first-time business owner found himself out of work and financially devastated

"I thought I was going to lose my house," reveals Travis. "I had literally started looking for sites I could park my camper. It had gotten that bad."

Desperate to stay afloat, Travis returned to his first love: teaching guitar. Although it had been almost three decades since he set foot in the classroom, he discovered that not much had changed. The "two-month hump" was still very much alive and well.

One afternoon while struggling to teach his daughter Bradi how to play, Travis shared his longtime dream of creating Chord-Buddy. Not only did she love the idea, she offered him a challenge. "If you create it," Bradi said, "I promise I'll learn how to play."

Seventeen prototypes and $1 million later, the music lover turned his dream into a reality. The ChordBuddy was officially born.

Interested in growing the brand and building the business, Travis went on *Shark Tank* and landed a deal with Robert Herjavec. Almost overnight, the ChordBuddy took off. But Travis knew the hard work wasn't over; it had just begun.

"You're never really over the hill," says Travis. "A lot of people view *Shark Tank* as the be all and end all, but I viewed it as a stepping-stone. I knew the spike would eventually go away, and I'd have to keep selling."

More than a year after Travis's episode aired, his business is still booming. With a new ChordBuddy Junior set to hit shelves by the end of 2013 and other exciting products on the way, Travis continues to share his love of the guitar with the world.

"It's amazing what ten minutes and forty two seconds in front of ten million people can do. It changed my life forever."

To find out more about ChordBuddy, visit ChordBuddy.com or follow them on Twitter @ChordBuddy.

REAL-WORLD WISDOM: "Always make sure you have a solid game plan and great advisors. Each part of the business building process is expensive, so you don't want to run and gun it. It's important to always be as prepared as possible."

PART TWO
SETTING UP SHOP

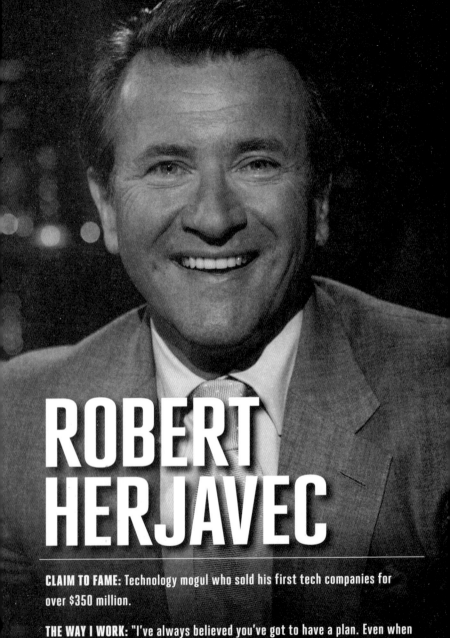

ROBERT HERJAVEC

CLAIM TO FAME: Technology mogul who sold his first tech companies for over $350 million.

THE WAY I WORK: "I've always believed you've got to have a plan. Even when my company was small and just starting out, we always had a target for what we were going to do each year."

THE UNLIKELY
ENTREPRENEUR

I never wanted to start my own business; I never wanted to be an entrepreneur. I just wanted to be happy and work for someone else. In fact, I only started my first company because I was fired from my job and couldn't find another one in time to pay the mortgage.

At the time, I was running a high-tech company and had just gotten married. When I returned from my honeymoon, the venture capitalist who'd funded the company had packed up all my things. I was fired, he told me, and his son was now going to be the president. Plus, he said that if I didn't stay on and run the sales department, he was going to claim I defrauded the company and sue me for $5 million. I left anyway.

When I got home and told my wife, she immediately started crying. Just then, we heard a knock on the door—it was the bailiff serving us with a writ for $5 million. I had never been fired; I had never been sued; and I had only been married for one day. It was awful. But I'll tell you what, that's the beauty of life. You have to look for the opportunities that let you do great things. And that's what it was: an opportunity. I could have either felt really miserable for myself or I could have shaken myself off and kept going. I chose to keep going.

I decided to start my first business, but not only that, I taught myself law too. I didn't have the money to hire a lawyer, and I didn't want to give the guy who fired me the satisfaction of knowing I was burning money on legal fees. So I worked on the business all day and taught myself law in the evening. I defended myself and took it all the way to the highest level court. It's amazing what you can learn when you have to learn it.

What I love about being on *Shark Tank* is that I get to meet a lot of people who share my belief—people who have a dream and who are waking up each day and trying to do better for themselves. You know, the world rewards substance. *Shark Tank* has really reaffirmed that idea for me.

4

FINDING YOUR CUSTOMERS

After assessing your entrepreneurial potential and evaluating your business idea, you probably have a good sense of what you're trying to create. But one fundamental question still remains: Who exactly are you selling *to*? Who makes up your target market?

A target market is the specific group of customers that your business aims to attract. Understanding yours will serve you throughout the business-building process.

Naturally, many new business owners are hungry for customers and will seek out just about anyone willing to buy their products or services. Although this strategy may sound intuitive, trying to appeal to an unfocused group of people can be ineffective. Instead, targeting your product or service to a niche audience will help build a more relevant, compelling, and sustainable business.

Let's say, for instance, that you've created a new natural and organic cosmetics line. Your initial instinct may be to target anyone who purchases makeup. But in reality that may not be the smartest move. The cosmetics space is oversaturated and dominated by large corporations with an abundance of resources. Selling your product to "women who wear makeup" would be like opening a restaurant for people who eat food. It's difficult to compete if you're competing with everyone.

Rather than aiming for any woman who buys makeup, it would be far more effective to focus on health-conscious women aged twenty-five to thirty-five who make more than $50,000 a year and live in major metropolitan areas. Yes, you've eliminated a large portion of the market, but now you can position your product in a way that deeply resonates with your ideal customer—instead of only being slightly relevant to everyone.

When defining your target market, there are five things to examine: demographic information, geographic location, wants and needs, hobbies and activities, and overall market size.

Demographic information: Identifying the age, gender, ethnicity, income level, and family status of your consumer is the first step to defining your target market. A product that appeals to an twenty-one-year-old white male making $22,000 a year and living at home will likely be quite different than one that appeals to a forty-five-year-old Hispanic female with two children making $150,000 a year. What demographic is the best fit for your business? This question is the starting point to better understanding your target market.

Geographic location: If your consumer lives in a rural area in the Deep South, she will probably have different needs than her urban-dwelling Northern counterpart. Likewise, a person who resides in the suburbs, rather than say a bustling city environment, may buy products through different channels. The only way to sell to your consumers is to know where to look for them.

Wants and needs: What does your consumer want and need? Those, by the way, are two very different things. Is he looking to upgrade his lifestyle? Is she trying to save for her child's college? Understanding what exactly your consumers are looking for will help you better identify their buying habits and position your business accordingly.

Hobbies and activities: Where do your customers hang out? What do they do for fun? Would they rather go to yoga on Saturday afternoon or spend the day at the local sports bar watching the game? Are they involved in their community, or do they prefer to keep to themselves? Try to get as specific as possible.

Market size: Roughly how large is the target market you're going after? If you're trying to sell to plumbers who live in Milwaukee with a net worth of more than $250,000, your model and strategy will look very different than if you're trying to target plumbers who live in Wisconsin with a net worth of more than $25,000. Do a little digging and try to acquire some basic information on the size of your market.

Finding your audience can be challenging, and sometimes there's no better way than to hit the streets and begin talking to everyone, at least that was ReadeREST founder Rick Hopper's strategy.

"I spent the first few months trying to figure out who my customers were," says Rick. "I got a trade show booth and set it up at every kind of show you could imagine: gun shows, craft shows, car shows. I tried to do at least three or four shows a month and get in front of as many people as I could. I knew it was the only way I'd discover my target market."

Defining a market can make many first-time entrepreneurs uncomfortable. But remember: just because you're targeting one type of consumer, doesn't mean you can't or won't appeal to others. You're simply focusing your efforts to have the maximum impact in the marketplace. What's more, your target

"When you sell a product or service, you're making a promise to your audience. If you don't understand your audience, you'll never be able to keep that promise and you'll ultimately let them down."

DAYMOND

market will likely change and grow with your business. Think of it as a formula. Until you get it just right, you'll want to regularly tinker with the variables.

Once you start acquiring this type of data, you may find it necessary to go back and refine your offerings. That's a good thing. Don't be afraid to use the facts you uncover to build a more targeted and effective business. That's what this kind of research is for.

IDENTIFYING THE COMPETITION

There are hundreds of different kinds of breakfast cereal sold in the United States, from sugary and unhealthy to wholesome and hearty. While many of these brands are owned by a handful of companies, that's still a lot of competition. It would be natural then for the first-time business owner to presume it's a wise idea to stay out of the cereal business. But that assumption may not necessarily be correct.

It's safe to bet that a family purchases more than one brand of cereal per household. Assuming each member of the family tries a few new brands every year, your cereal may actually stand a fighting chance—that is, if you find a way to make it onto grocery store shelves.

Competition should be welcomed, not feared. In fact, being first to market is rarely a good thing. When you're first, you often must take on the responsibility of educating the consumer, which can be a costly and time-consuming task. If you've invented the first time machine, for instance, you must prove the value not only of your product, but of the entire product category as well. In other words, before you can sell a single time machine, you must teach your customers why they need the device in the first place. That's a lot of work just to sell one lousy time machine. Competition not only saves you from this resource-draining task, it proves there's already a demand for your product or service.

Because the average American family buys cereal, you can assume that pretty much everyone understands the value of the product. Therefore, if you create the next great cereal, you need only convince consumers that *your* cereal is the best. And that process starts by researching the key players in your industry.

In the past, finding your competitors wasn't always an easy task. Thanks to technology, however, the world is far more transparent than ever before. When trying to assess your competitive landscape, you'll want to come up with a strategy that combines both online and offline efforts. Below are a few quick ways to get started:

Harness the power of Google: Of course the obvious first step is to search for your competition on the Internet. That's a given. But outside of just your basic search, Google has a variety of tools that can help add additional value to your quest. By setting Google Alerts to receive news about your competitors and topics related to your business, you can stay up-to-date on the latest happenings in your industry. With Google Analytics, you can track your website's traffic, including where visitors came from and where they went when they left. Not only are these tools extremely helpful, they're also free and easy to access.

To set up Google Alerts, visit Google.com/Alerts. From there, simply type in any word you wish to be notified about. If you own a cupcake bakery, for example, like Wicked Good Cupcake founder Tracey Noonan does, you may wish to select keywords like "cupcake" or "Boston bakery." Once you've chosen the appropriate words, simply select which type of content you'd like to receive notification of and how often you'd like to receive it. That's all it takes! Once the alert has been created, you'll begin getting regular notifications in your inbox. Setting up Google Analytics is a bit more complicated and requires syncing your Google account with your website. To get step-by-step instructions on this process, visit Google .com/Analytics

Explore social media: Social media can be a powerful marketing tool. It can also be a great way to keep an eye on your competitor. You needn't be a technology expert to see what other companies are doing on Twitter, Facebook, and LinkedIn. Spend a few minutes each day exploring these sites. You'd be shocked at what 140 characters can reveal.

Attend trade shows and conferences: One of the best ways to stay updated on the latest innovations and advances in your industry is to attend trade shows and conferences. These events are great not only for networking, but also for keeping tabs on your competitors. Steep ticket prices may prevent you from attending every trade show or conference, but it's worth budgeting a little money each year for these types of events. Don't forget, they're tax-deductible.

Chat with customers: Some of the best intel can be found from those closest to you. There's a good chance your current or prospective customers have interacted with your competi-

"You have to be willing to work hard. There are no shortcuts to running a business. Every business has competition and your competitors are always looking for ways to beat you to the punch. You have to find ways to make your company stronger every day."

MARK

tors at some point over the years. While you should never put them in an uncomfortable position, asking the occasional pointed question isn't inappropriate. Be smart about it though. Your business relies on these relationships, and you don't want to do anything that jeopardizes them.

Visit your competitors: Depending on your specific type of business, you may be able to actually pay your competitors a visit. This is limited mainly to companies that have retail locations open to consumers. If you own a spa, for instance, it wouldn't hurt to book an afternoon of services with another spa in town. This is often the best way to gain insight into things like customer service and company culture.

Don't be discouraged if you discover you have more competition than you initially thought. Competition not only forces you to work harder and be more creative, it dramatically expedites the innovation process. Instead of using your competition as a reason *not* to start your business, let it push you that much further.

PICKING THE PERFECT NAME

Naming your company is one of the most important decisions you'll make in the start-up phase. Not only does the name you choose influence everything from your trademark to your Web properties, but it also plays an integral role in your brand.

A superior name should leave a lasting impression and communicate the very essence of your company. It should be distinct enough to make an impact, but broad enough to allow for some degree of flexibility. Moreover, a great name shouldn't just be catchy and memorable, it should be an extension of your story—a reflection of your products and services.

Perhaps the greatest challenge in the naming process is a lack of definitive rules. For every expert opinion you find on the subject, there are a slew of groundbreaking companies that have gone against the grain and created something exceptional. There are however a few general guidelines to consider as you begin the brainstorming process:

Make it easy to remember: It may sound obvious, but plenty of companies forget how important a memorable name can be. No matter your business, you'll likely enter a marketplace that is rife with competition. Creating a name that's easy to remember can provide a competitive advantage that may otherwise be difficult to attain. Example: Painted Pretzel, *Shark Tank* Season 3.

Avoid local names: While entrepreneurs should serve their community, giving your company a local name isn't advised. If you own a hardware store in Tampa, for instance, it wouldn't be wise to name your business Tampa Bay Hardware. There's always the potential your business may grow, and using a local name can cause complications down the line. If Tampa Bay Hardware opened a store in Miami, for example, they would either have to call the store Miami Hardware, which would damage the overall brand identity, or use the original name, which might be confusing to Miami residents. Unless you have absolutely no plans whatsoever to grow the business outside your immediate area, it's best to avoid using a local name.

Keep it simple: If your business has more than six or seven syllables or words, you may want to go back to the drawing board. Your name doesn't have to be complicated to be memorable. Example: eCreamery, *Shark Tank* Season 4.

Stay away from strange spelling and made-up words: Names like Kwik and Kourteous House Repairs and EZ Dry Cleaning may sound clever, but strange spellings or made-up words can actually end up doing your company a great disservice. Since many people use search engines to find businesses, especially local businesses, having a complicated name that's difficult to spell may end up costing you customers.

Put yourself in your customer's shoes: It's easy to get distracted by a name that has great significance to you but no one else. Don't forget to consider your customer when brainstorming. Of course your company's name should be meaningful to you, but it's even more important that it has a clear meaning to your customer. Example: Game Face, *Shark Tank* Season 4.

Test it out: Once you've come up with a few different options, test them out on potential customers and colleagues. Your family and friends may also be able to offer some valuable feedback, but keep in mind that they may not approach the task with the objectivity and honesty you need. Be sure to test your ideas with a wide spectrum of people who accurately represent your target market, and incorporate any useful feedback.

Once you've decided on a few potential options, the next step is to check the U.S. Patent Office's website to see if any of your potential names are legally available. With hundreds

"Not only is a good name catchy and memorable, it should help people understand what your business does. Today's world is all about the Google search. If your name reflects your products or services, you'll have a much better chance of being found, so it's important to choose wisely."

LORI

of thousands of trademarks registered each year, some of your ideas may already be in use. You'll read more about patents, trademarks, and copyrights in Chapter Six.

Finally, you'll want to search online to see which domain names are available. It's very likely the .com suffix for your company name will already be taken, so you may need to get creative with your domain name. Make sure you don't get *too* creative though. You'll eventually market your business online, and you'll want to have a domain that's similar to your company's name. This would also be a good time to secure your username on Twitter and Facebook. You'll need those sooner than you think.

A great name is crucial to your business, so don't feel like you need to rush the process. Whether it's on the treadmill or in the office, budget a little time each day to brainstorm. Compile a list of competitors' names, search industry-related media, or find your own unique ways to spark inspiration. Whatever your process may be, don't forget that a great name has the potential to increase credibility, communicate a mission, and attract customers. And what could be better than that?

THE 60-SECOND TEST: WHAT'S YOUR VALUE?

Here's a test: in sixty seconds or less explain why your consumer should patronize your business, as opposed to your competitors'. What is the *specific* value you're offering and how does it differ from what's already in the marketplace?

How did you do? Did you pass the test? If so, congratulations. You have a basic understanding of your unique value proposition. If not, now is the time to figure it out.

A value proposition is a business statement that explains why a consumer should buy your product or service. And with a rapidly expanding marketplace, having a compelling value proposition is essential.

Your value proposition should be simple to understand and explain to others. In fact, the easier it is to remember, the more likely it is that your customers will share it with others.

If crafted well, your value proposition should accomplish five things:

- Differentiate the business
- Grow sales
- Create organic buzz
- Inspire consumer connection
- Demonstrate relevancy in the market

To get you thinking in the right direction, here's an example of a value proposition for a new sports drink called XYZ Beverage:

XYZ Beverage: Value Proposition

"Using only natural and organic ingredients that people can actually pronounce, XYZ Beverage offers all the electrolytes and potassium of a leading sports drink without all the sugar and sodium. Our philosophy is simple: give athletes more of the stuff they want and less of the stuff they don't. Simple, healthy, and delicious—now that's something worth working for."

In only three sentences, the XYZ Beverage Company both demonstrated their value and differentiated themselves from the competition. Let's examine their value proposition line by line.

Using only natural and organic ingredients that people can actually pronounce, XYZ Beverage offers all the electrolytes and potassium of a leading sports drink without all the sugar and sodium.

Sports drinks are notorious for being filled with sugar, sodium, and other foreign ingredients. From the very beginning XYZ Beverage is proving they're different from the rest by being transparent and honest about their ingredients.

Our philosophy is simple: give athletes more of the stuff they want and less of the stuff they don't.

By including their philosophy in their value proposition, they're humanizing their business and subtly showing that their company is centered on values and beliefs.

Simple, healthy, and delicious—now that's something worth working for.

Athletes, their target market, are by nature goal-oriented. By using the verbiage "that's something worth working for," they're establishing a connection with their consumer. They're saying, "Hey look! We're just like you."

Spend some time creating your value proposition, and don't be afraid to reach out to customers, friends, family, and coworkers. Find out what sorts of things they're looking for in a product or service like yours. It's likely you'll discover a few things you have never considered.

5

GETTING DOWN TO BUSINESS

I t isn't just about what you do; it's about why you do it. In fact, your company's mission can become your most powerful differentiator.

Take Donny McCall, for instance, who appeared on Season 3 of *Shark Tank*. His product Invis-a-Rack quickly and effortlessly turns an everyday pickup truck into a cargo management system by providing a functional ladder rack that can be collapsed down into the bed rail casings. When McCall pitched to the Sharks, he voiced a steadfast commitment to continue making his product in the United States. Concerned as he was about the loss of manufacturing jobs in America, keeping production domestic was more than just a desire for McCall; it was part of his company's mission. Although it ended up costing him a deal with the Sharks, Donny and his company received a surge of positive support and feedback. Eventually, thanks in part to his mission, Donny signed a deal with Iowa-based truck accessory giant Dee Zee. Today, his product is stronger than ever, and he's fulfilled his commitment to keep manufacturing in the United States. Mission matters.

With the abundance of tasks a new business owner faces, it's easy to forget just how valuable a strong mission can be, but it's an element you simply cannot afford to overlook. What does your company stand for? Who are you trying to serve? What drives you each and every day?

The first step in developing a strong mission is to create a mission statement, a short summary that explains both what you do and why you do it. What's more, it highlights your company's commitments to its customers and partners. Here are a few things to consider when writing your mission statement:

Keep it brief: Remember, it's a statement. One to three well-crafted sentences is all it should take to express your mission in an honest, compelling, and thoughtful way.

Avoid superlatives: It's natural to want to share just how fantastic your business is with the world. But save that for the press release. A mission statement should be a summary of your mission, not of your excellence.

Borrow inspiration: If you're having trouble getting started, read the mission statements of companies you love. If they've won you over, it's likely they have a strong mission. Try to pinpoint why their statements resonate and use those findings as inspiration for your own.

Ask around: Don't be afraid to test your mission statement.

SHARK BITE

"You have to know your personal mission and your mission as a company. If you don't, you leave it up to others to interpret. Mission was core when I started FUBU: for us, by us. We wanted to dress the consumer that was being neglected. It wasn't about a color; it was about a generation. Our mission was clear."

DAYMOND

Sometimes stepping back and allowing others to weigh in can provide a level of perspective you can't achieve on your own.

Once you've created your mission statement, make sure it's fully accessible to your customers and team. It won't serve your business if it's tucked out of sight. Put it on your website, hang it in your store, and make it a central part of your company's culture.

BUILDING CORE VALUES

If a mission statement provides a high-level overview of your company's philosophy, then core values are the guiding principles that help you achieve it. These simple but powerful bylaws usually come straight from the founder and influence everything from management style to which vendors a company chooses to work with. By spotlighting your company's beliefs, your core values will serve a fundamental role in all aspects of your business.

While it's helpful for your customers to be aware of your core values, it's absolutely critical that your team—from sales and accounting to HR and operations—understands these values and infuses them in every action they take.

Keep in mind that while building core values should be in the back of your mind from the start, it's likely they'll develop slowly over time. The truth is, outside of your initial idea for a business, you probably don't know a lot about your new venture. That's natural at this stage in the game. Don't ignore core values, but don't force them either.

When you are thinking about your core values, here are six central areas you may wish to focus on:

Employees: What role do you envision your employees playing in your business? Will you invest in their personal growth and development outside the office? Is empowerment an important part of your philosophy? Even if you don't currently have a team, take a minute to think about these questions.

Customers: How do you treat your customers? What should they expect from you? What should you expect from them? Building a strong and loyal customer base is every entrepreneur's dream. Spend some time imagining what that relationship looks like.

Vendors: How do you choose your vendors? Who's your ideal vendor? Why should your customer trust your vendors? Whether you like it or not, the suppliers, distributors, and other vendors you choose to work with are an extension of your business. Don't forget to acknowledge that relationship.

Product or service: How do you ensure a high-quality product or service? How much time and energy goes into each of your offerings? How vital is your product and service to the success of your business? Core values should express your commitment to building a superior product or service with transparency and authenticity.

Culture: Does your culture breed excitement and innovation? Do your employees look forward to coming to work on Monday mornings? Have you spent time and care creating a first-class work environment? How does culture affect the day-to-day operations of your business?

Impact: How does your company make a difference? Do you regularly support charitable causes or organizations? Do you champion a social mission? One of the best ways to have an impact in the *market* is to understand how your business can have an impact in the *world*.

Core values are another one of those small details that can easily be ignored or forgotten. But as a business owner, it's up to you to make sure they get the attention they deserve. Spend

BARBARA

"You learn core values along the way by doing. With my own business, for example, if you had asked me what my core values were within the first two years, I would have had no idea. But within a few years, I'd learned that our business is all about a collaborative effort and having fun. And that leads to innovation. The more fun we had, the more we were willing to innovate."

as much time as you need crafting them, and when you're ready, share them proudly with your employees, customers, and partners. You never know, your core values may just end up being the legacy you leave behind.

DEVELOPING YOUR BUSINESS MODEL

If you're a regular *Shark Tank* viewer, you may know more about business models than you think, particularly which ones work and which ones do not.

In its most basic form, a business model is how a company makes money. More specifically, it describes how an organization creates, delivers, and captures value. Business models can range in detail and complexity, but a study done by the Massachusetts Institute of Technology Sloan School of Management in 2004 discovered that almost every model falls under one of four main archetypes:

Creator: A creator "buys raw materials or components from suppliers and then transforms or assembles them to create a product sold to buyers." Pretty much any manufacturing operation would fall under this category. EXAMPLE: Daymond John's company FUBU.

Distributor: A distributor "buys a product and resells essentially the same product to someone else." While a distributor may add additional value somewhere throughout the distribution cycle, essentially he is selling a product that already exists. EXAMPLE: Any of the products Lori Greiner sells on QVC.

Landlord: The landlord "sells the right to use, but not own, an asset for a specified period of time." Any rental business operates under this archetype. EXAMPLE: Mark Cuban's company Magnolia Pictures, which gives movie theaters limited rights to show their films.

Broker: The broker "facilitates sales by matching potential buyers and sellers." The broker doesn't actually own anything, rather she facilitates a transaction. EXAMPLE: Barbara Corcoran's former company The Corcoran Group.

Now that you understand the four basic archetypes, it's time to start thinking about developing your own business model.

A 2001 study published by Accenture—a highly regarded global consulting firm—examined business models from seventy different companies. The good news (and perhaps also the bad news) is that their study confirmed there isn't one surefire model guaranteed to bring in cash. From timing to technology, many factors play a role in the success of a business model. They did however uncover three characteristics that were prevalent in every good model.

First, *a solid business model offers unique value.* While this could include the invention of a new product or service, it doesn't have to. Providing unique value can be about providing a new or different feature that delights the consumer.

Next, *the business model must be difficult to imitate.* When a company finds a creative way to stand out, it creates barriers to entry that prevent other businesses from competing.

SHARK BITE

"Having the ability to be brutally honest with yourself is the greatest challenge you face when creating a business model. Too often we oversell ourselves on the quality of the idea, service, or product. We don't provide an honest assessment of how we fit in the market, why customers will buy from us, and at what price. It's a reason many entrepreneurs fail."

MARK

And finally, *a strong business model should be grounded in reality.* Although they may not admit it, many companies lack awareness about where and how they make their money. This is particularly true in larger organizations. A good business model is grounded in reality and takes into account accurate information about cost, revenue, and consumer behavior.

When creating your business model, don't forget to fully examine your market size, consumer segment, and competition. The more data you can gather, the better your model will be. When you find a model that works, by all means stick to it! But keep in mind that business models aren't static; they often evolve and shift as your company does the same.

SETTING YOUR PRICE

Let's say you're on vacation and want to buy a bottle of water. Now, you could purchase one at the local drugstore for $1, or at the coffee shop for $3, or the theme park for $5. You're welcome to take the bottle of water that's sitting in your hotel room, but that will cost you $7, or you could wait until you go to that fancy restaurant for dinner and order a bottle of sparkling water for $12. No matter how much you decide to shell out, you're basically getting the same product: water, aqua, H20. So why does the cost vary so dramatically? Because each establishment has developed its own pricing strategy based on a detailed set of criteria.

Before you can decide how much you'll charge for a product or service, you must take into account everything from market to consumer to competition. As with business models, there are many strategies to consider—more than twenty popular ones—but here are five of the most common pricing strategies you'll encounter:

Cost-plus pricing: By far the most basic, cost-plus pricing combines the price of producing a product with the percentage of profit the company wishes to make. The result of that equation is the selling price. Let's say, for instance, that your variable costs (materials, labor, production) come to $8 per unit while your fixed costs are $12 per unit, totaling $20 in cost. To make a steady profit, you want to operate at a 30 percent markup, so you add an additional $6 to the cost, which gives you a total selling price of $26.

Although this model may sound like the simplest way to ensure profitability, its simplicity can also be its downfall. The problem with cost-plus pricing is that it doesn't take into account important factors like demand and competition. Without having more information about the market, it's difficult to know if your product or service will be able to actively compete.

Value-based pricing: An effective choice for both product and service businesses, this strategy is based on the perception of value your product or service provides, not on any actual production costs. Take, for example, the eyewear industry. Whether you charge $50 or $500 for a pair of sunglasses, the production cost varies only slightly. You don't pay $500 for a pair of sunglasses because the materials cost ten times as much. No, what you're paying for is the perceived value of those sunglasses (e.g., the belief that you'll look more fashionable). For this pricing strategy to be effective you must have an in-depth knowledge of your market.

Price skimming: Most business owners think that for profit to be high, the volume of sales must also be high. But that's not always the case. Price skimming works the opposite way: relatively lower sales at a higher profit. A good example of this would be a boutique consulting firm. Instead of trying to secure ten clients at $10,000 an engagement, under this strategy the business owner would seek to gain four clients at a $25,000 price point.

Why would anyone want to adopt a strategy that assumes lower sales? Depending on your business, having fewer customers that spend more money might actually be a better solution. Not only do you create more exclusivity for your brand, the clientele you attract generally tends to become better customers. Of course, the danger with this strategy is that losing a handful of customers at the wrong time can greatly impact your organization. Still, it can be the ideal choice for certain types of businesses, especially service-based companies with premium offerings and deeply loyal consumers.

Penetration pricing: Sign up now and get twelve months of high-speed Internet service for only $29.99 a month. Sound familiar? That's a perfect example of penetration pricing. Using this strategy, a business sets low initial rates in order to gain market share and then eventually raises prices. That promise of twelve months of cheap Internet usually comes with the caveat that you sign a two-year contract. And chances are, the second year will be billed at a significantly higher rate than the first. The key to effectively using this pricing strategy is to be transparent from the start. It's not smart to hike up your

SHARK BITE

"The price of anything is relative to the price of something else, which means you better know the price of everything you're competing against. And that isn't always obvious. It's not about how much profit you need to make; it's about what the market will bear for your product or service, relative to something else."

ROBERT

rates without warning your customers in advance. Remember what happened when Netflix did that?

Psychological pricing: Let's go back to the example of twelve months of high-speed Internet service for only $29.99 a month. Would that deal have been as appealing if offered for $30.00 a month? Experts aren't so sure. Psychological pricing assumes that certain price points—usually just a few pennies short of the dollar—have a more favorable psychological impact.

For many, the first instinct when thinking about pricing is to charge as little as possible. But that's not always the best way to go. Undercutting your competition for the sake of short-term gain can be damaging to both your business and industry. The race to the bottom is a quick one, and before you know it you'll have put yourself out of business. Instead, the smarter choice is to develop a keen understanding of your market and create a pricing strategy that will help your business achieve sustainable growth.

WRITING A BUSINESS PLAN

A business plan, in its simplest form, outlines the goals of a business and the steps required to achieve them.

A business plan can be as long or as short as you want. It can be scribbled on the back of a napkin or laid out with thought and care. It can be presented to a team of investors or shared with nobody at all. But even though your business plan can take on whatever shape you'd like it to, there is a fairly specific template that most people choose to follow:

Executive summary: This is a clear statement that summarizes the overall business. Essentially it's a bird's-eye view of the what, why, and how of your business.

Business description: The business description is a basic overview of your industry, markets, and business. It should include information about your target audience and how you'll differentiate yourself in the marketplace.

Market analysis: While the business description is very high-level, this section details your business's target market and the industry as a whole.

Competitor analysis: The competitor analysis offers a snapshot of the competitive landscape, including competitors' strengths and weaknesses, potential barriers to entry, and strategies to stand out.

Marketing plan: This plan will provide a detailed outline of the pricing strategy, sales plan, and advertising and promotion activities. It should describe how you'll get your product to consumers and bring in business.

Management plan: The management plan is a description of the legal structure of your business, roles and responsibilities of the management team, and any additional human resources needs you may require.

Operating plan: This should outline your daily operational strategy, including location, employment needs, manufacturing process, and inventory requirements.

Financial plan: The financial plan provides a detailed breakdown of your business's financial data, including funding requirements and financial analysis.

When putting together a traditional business plan try to keep it around twenty to thirty pages in length. While business plans have traditionally been longer, today the trend is for a quicker and simpler approach. In other words, get to the point. It's also important to add any appropriate visual elements (graphs, charts, etc.). Image matters, and a poorly laid out business plan is not the best way to get attention, at least not the kind of attention you want.

The challenge with this type of business plan is that today's startups have the ability to test their ideas and adjust their strategy more rapidly than ever before. The more traditional business plan just doesn't leave a lot of room for flexibility and alteration. Furthermore, most entrepreneurs would rather use the time it takes to write an elaborate business plan to actually test their idea. So in the last few years, numerous other approaches have been invented. From Eric Ries's Lean Model Canvas to David Madié's Growth Wheel, business experts from a variety of backgrounds have begun to offer plans that reflect the real challenges a new business faces.

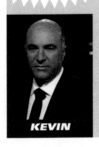

SHARK BITE

"It's always good to have a roadmap, but keep in mind that it's going to change dramatically by the time success is achieved. That's why business plans don't carry much weight for me as an investor. I'm more interested in the team behind the plan."

KEVIN

Whether you choose to create a classic business plan or explore a more modern approach, it is important that you have a clear way forward. You wouldn't explore new territory without a road map, and you shouldn't launch a new venture without some sort of plan. To find examples of a few thoughtful business plans, flip to the Tools and Resources section in the back of this book.

MARGINS OF SUCCESS: UNDERSTANDING PROFIT

In an episode of *Shark Tank* it's not uncommon for one of the Sharks to ask, "What are the margins like for your product?" Some entrepreneurs are prepared with this information, while others struggle to even comprehend the question. When it's discussed on the show, the Shark is usually referring to gross profit, not net profit. There's a difference.

Gross profit is the net sales minus the cost of goods and services sold. To determine gross profit margins you need only follow this simple formula:

Selling price – cost of product ÷ by selling price × 100 = ?%

So, for instance, if you sell your product for $100 and it costs $50 to make, the formula would look like this: $100 (selling price) – $50 (cost of product) = $50 ÷ 100 (selling price) = .5 × 100 = 50%.

In the above example, your profit margin would be 50%.

Net profit on the other hand is the profit you make after all expenses that were not included in the calculation of gross profit have been paid (rent, utilities, etc.). You'll learn more about fixed and variable costs in Part Three of the book.

When it comes to determining profit margin, there isn't a set of standardized best practices. On the contrary, many factors play a role in the process, including industry, location, and overhead. While a 10 percent margin may be acceptable in some industries, the standard for others may be closer to 40 or 50 percent. There are plenty of resources online, such as BizStats.com, that provide information on average profit margins for specific industries.

As you begin thinking about your pricing strategy, especially if you eventually plan on seeking additional funding, understanding how to calculate and discuss profit margin is absolutely crucial. The more information you can arm yourself with, the better off you'll be.

6

MAKING IT OFFICIAL

I ntroducing the government to your new venture is an essential step toward taking your idea from concept to creation. But before you can do that, you must first decide how your business will be organized and which type of legal structure is the best fit. Luckily, your options are fairly limited. In fact, there are really only four basic legal structures to consider:

- Sole proprietorship
- Partnership
- Limited liability company (LLC)
- Corporation

Deciding which type of incorporation status you'll seek may seem like a small decision, but it will play a pivotal role in how you start and run your business. It can also greatly affect how much money you'll owe the IRS at tax time.

"The importance of incorporating is something that a lot of entrepreneurs don't learn until it's too late," says Moshe Weiss, founder of SoundBender, who appeared on Season 4 of *Shark Tank*. "You could file as one type of entity and all of the sudden owe the government $20,000, which could have been avoided if you had just filed differently."

The basic legal structure you choose depends primarily on two key pieces of information: how much liability you wish to take on and how many people will own the business. Once you know that information, deciding which form of incorporation to select is a fairly straightforward task. Still, it's important to understand the benefits and implications of each:

Sole proprietorship: Believe it or not, you may already own a sole proprietorship and not even know it. According to the United States government, a sole proprietorship, also referred to as a "sole trader" or "proprietorship," is an unincorporated business that is owned and run by one individual, with no distinction between the business and the owner. A freelance photographer or nanny, for instance, is by default a sole proprietor.

Since the individual is the sole beneficiary of the business, it is he who is personally responsible for both the profits and the losses. Therefore, when it's time to pay taxes, it's not necessary to file a separate business return; all income is reported directly on the entrepreneur's personal tax return.

Keep in mind that many states require most sole proprietorships to acquire certain permits and licenses, depending on the type of business. Research what kind of documentation your business may require—even if it's already up and running. Otherwise, you could face a major headache later.

Those who wish to operate a sole proprietorship under a different name than their own (e.g., Mary's Day Care Services instead of simply Mary Smith) can file for a "fictitious name," most often referred to as a DBA ("doing business as"). While a sole proprietorship is perhaps the easiest and least expensive way to start a business, it's not the right choice for every new venture.

Because there is no legal separation between the business owner and the business itself in a sole proprietorship, the entrepreneur is responsible for all business debts and obligations. Let's say, for instance, that a client decides to file suit against Mary's Day Care Services. If the organization is set up as a sole proprietorship, the plaintiff can go after both Mary's business and personal assets. This alone makes the sole proprietorship less than ideal for many new business owners.

Partnership: Not every new entrepreneur is ready to start a company on her own. For some, it's better to get in business with a person whom they trust and respect. No matter which state you reside in, there are only three different types of partnerships:

General partnership: Widely considered the most common partnership, in a general partnership all of the profits, management, and liabilities are shared equally between partners.

Limited partnership: Ideal for ventures backed by partners who are making different investment commitments, in a limited partnership profits, management, and liabilities are limited instead of shared equally.

Joint venture: Similar to a general partnerships, in a joint venture profits, management, and liabilities are shared equally among partners, but only for a specified amount of time.

No matter which type of partnership you choose to form, the first step should be to draw up a partnership agreement that lays out the specific details of your working relationship and describes how general business decisions will be made. Although a partnership agreement isn't legally required, it's highly recommend.

As with any kind of partnership, especially a legally recognized one, you should think carefully about whom you wish to align yourself with. Similar to a sole proprietorship, a partnership does not legally separate a business from the owner. This means, for instance, that if your partner makes an unwise financial decision, you too will be responsible for the repercussions. What's more, under United States law, all partners can be sued for the full amount of any business debt—not just their share. So if your company was sued for $10,000, either partner could be responsible for the full $10,000.

To form a partnership, you must first register with the state and establish your business name. You should also register with the IRS and apply for a federal tax ID number. While partnerships do not have to pay additional business taxes, they are required to report all losses and gains by filing an "informational return" (Form 1065).

Limited Liability Company (LLC): For many, the idea of being personally liable for business obligations automatically eliminates sole proprietorships and partnerships from the equation. On the other hand, the implications of starting a full-fledged corporation can feel daunting. This is when the limited liability company (LLC) makes the most sense. An LLC combines the best of both worlds: limited personal liability, straightforward tax requirements, and maximum flexibility.

In an LLC, there are no "owners" but instead "members," who can range from a single individual to a corporation, depending on the state. As in sole proprietorships and partnerships, members must report profits and losses on their personal tax returns and are not taxed as a separate business entity.

Starting an LLC is fairly straightforward. While each state is slightly different, the process generally requires choosing a unique business name and filing articles of incorporation with the secretary of state. Depending on your type of business, you may also need to acquire certain licenses and permits, and in some states, including New York and Arizona, you must announce your business in a local paper. As with a partnership, when starting an LLC with more than one member, it's best to draft an operating agreement.

Corporation: If you're looking for maximum protection and the largest variety of tax and fringe benefits, like stock options and retirement, the corporation is your best bet. Similar to an LLC, a corporation absolves its owners from all (or at least the majority of) personal liability, making it an attractive choice.

A corporation is an independent legal entity that is separate from its owners, who are also known as shareholders. In a private corporation (i.e., one that is not traded on the stock market), shares are issued to a select individual or group of individuals. Conversely, anyone can purchase shares of a public corporation on the stock market. It's important to note here that publicly traded corporations are a different beast altogether. For the sake of this book, it's assumed that if you're interested in starting a corporation, it will be private, not public.

A primary differentiator between a corporation and any of the other legal structures discussed thus far is the tax requirements, which change slightly depending on which specific type of corporation you file under:

C corporation: This is the most common type of incorporation, and businesses that form under it must pay taxes on whatever profit remains after deducting employee compensation, fringe benefits, and various other appropriate expenses. The C corporation is the most time- and resource-intensive structure—but it also comes with the most benefits.

S corporation: Similar to the previous forms of incorporation, businesses that form under this legal structure do not pay taxes on the business itself—all profits pass through to the owners. You might wonder why a business would organize under an S corporation when they could just form an LLC. As you'll read later, there are certain tax benefits that come with the S corporation, and it's often a better choice if you're giving away equity. Still, the LLC is quickly becoming the more popular choice.

When choosing which incorporation status to seek, be sure to pick a structure that's within your price range and comfort level but that also can sufficiently protect and support your organization as it grows.

TANK TIP

"You've got to learn how to be honest with yourself about your business. Are you proud of it? Do you believe in what you're doing? I'm very proud of our company and what we do. That makes it so much easier to get out of bed every day. If you don't believe in what you're doing, you really shouldn't start the business."

—SABIN LOMAC, COFOUNDER OF COUSINS MAINE LOBSTER

PROTECTING YOUR IDEA

Perhaps you've come up with a wonderful idea. Maybe you've invented something profound, the likes of which the world has never seen. Your immediate instinct upon making such a thrilling discovery is probably to protect it—to keep your idea or invention safe from those who could steal it. That reaction is natural; you can find plenty of stories of businesses that were hijacked by their competition. But the reality is that most entrepreneurs spend far too much time *protecting* their idea and not enough time *perfecting* it.

We're living in the age of information, where ideas—even great ideas—are everywhere. You need only search the phrase "free business ideas" on the Internet to find tens of thousands of pages dedicated to the topic. From a website that ranks the quality of preschools to a smart fridge that automatically orders groceries, there are plenty of ideas floating around in cyberspace, just waiting for the right entrepreneur to come along and make them work. Because that's really what it comes down to: execution.

For example, how many different barbecue sauces have been invented in the last decade? Ten? Fifteen? Twenty-five? Probably far more than that. Barbecue isn't a new idea. And yet the founders of Pork Barrel BBQ, who appeared on Season Three of *Shark Tank* and struck a deal with Barbara Corcoran, have been able to do extremely well. Why is that? Is it the recipe? Perhaps. Was it their appearance on *Shark Tank*? Maybe. But they were already in one hundred stores before going into the tank. Brett Thompson and Heath Hall, the founders of Pork Barrel BBQ, have succeeded not just because they had a great idea, but because they were able to execute it with creativity and precision.

For many entrepreneurs like Brett and Heath, protecting an idea isn't essential. If you're opening an ice cream shop, for instance, you probably shouldn't spend countless resources protecting your recipe before you've even made your first batch. In fact, most business owners won't ever need to devote significant time or money to protecting their idea, because most businesses aren't selling anything proprietary.

There are, however, specific types of businesses where protecting a product can make all the difference. If you feel as though some part of your business is proprietary, below are three of the most popular ways of protecting intellectual property:

Patent: Granted to an inventor by the United States government, a patent excludes others from "making, using, offering for sale, or selling the invention throughout the United States or importing the invention into the United States." Not every idea is patentable. According to the United States Patent and Trademark Office, the laws of nature, physical phenomena, and abstract ideas cannot be patented. So, for example, it may be difficult to patent a piece of software that relies heavily on a mathematical algorithm. Patents generally range from fourteen to twenty years and carry with them various fees, depending on the specific kind of patent. While there are online resources to help inventors secure patents, the process can be exhausting and complicated. Most of the time it's worth spending the extra money to hire an attorney who specializes in the process. You'll learn more about patents later in this chapter.

Trademark: While a patent protects an idea, a trademark protects a brand or, more specifically, "a word, phrase, symbol, and/or design that identifies and distinguishes the source of the goods of one party from those of others." If you need to protect a service instead of goods, you'd seek a service mark, which, although slightly different, is often also referred to as a trademark. A trademark can be owned or licensed and must be actively maintained through lawful use to avoid abandonment of the mark. Basically, use it or lose it.

Copyright: If a trademark protects a brand, a copyright protects the content that brand creates or, according to the U.S. government, "works of authorship, such as writings, music, and works of art that have been tangibly expressed." You know the warning that flashes on the screen before you

SHARK BITE

"Entrepreneurs with unique products are wise to try to protect themselves with a good patent. Often when a company is successful, a competitor will try to knock off the idea or replicate the business model. As an entrepreneur, you put so much time and energy into getting a product to market. It feels great to be able to protect it."

LORI

watch a movie? That's enforcing a copyright. What most people don't know is that you needn't register a copyright for it to exist. A copyright is active from the very moment the content is created. You must register your copyright only if you want to go on record as the owner or you feel as though you may need to protect your copyright in a court of law. For most people, registering a copyright isn't necessary.

While the majority of entrepreneurs will spend little time dealing with any of this, intellectual property should be understood and taken seriously. Infringing on another party's intellectual property, even if accidental, can result in expensive punishment for you and your company—something many small business owners cannot afford to encounter. It's possible to navigate intellectual property issues on your own, but hiring a professional is usually the better choice.

PROTECTING YOUR BUSINESS

While entrepreneurs spend too much time protecting their ideas, they don't spend enough time protecting their business with the right insurance. A 2010 survey by Travelers

Insurance found that 94 percent of small business owners feel confident they are protected against "insurable risks that can result in significant financial losses or even cause you to go out of business altogether." But at the same time, only a little over half—56 percent—of that 94 percent had disaster recovery insurance.

Of the many expenditures an entrepreneur faces, insurance seems to be one of the most resented. And yet purchasing the right insurance can end up saving your business thousands or even millions of dollars. From data breach to workers' compensation, there are a plethora of different insurance options, but here are four of the most common types of business insurance that every entrepreneur should understand:

General liability insurance: If you only purchase one type of insurance, general liability is probably the most important one to get. This type of policy covers accidents, injuries, and, usually, claims of negligence. If somebody is injured on your property, for instance, this is the insurance you'll need. It's important to note that general liability insurance most often does not cover claims like wrongful termination, harassment, and discrimination.

Professional liability insurance: Also known as "errors and omissions," this insurance covers malpractice, errors, and negligence in the rendering of services to your customers. Some professionals, like physicians, are legally required to carry this type of insurance. If your business primarily provides services, as opposed to products, professional liability insurance is important to have.

Product liability insurance: If your business manufactures, distributes, or retails a product, this insurance is something you may wish to consider. It protects the company against any financial loss accrued from a defective product that causes injury or bodily harm.

Property insurance: Property insurance covers more than just damage to the physical property; it covers everything related to the loss and damage of that property, including business interruption and loss of income. There are two types of property insurance policies: peril-specific and all-risk policies. Unless your business is in a particularly high-risk area for certain types of natural disasters, the all-risk policy is most likely all you need. If you run your business from home, keep in mind that most home owner policies do not cover home-based business losses. For that, you'll want to explore specific home-based business insurance policies.

Now the big question: How much insurance do you actually need? Unfortunately, there isn't a one-size-fits-all answer. If you own a construction company, for instance, you probably need more liability insurance than a photographer. If you've purchased a new office, you'll want to take out more property insurance than somebody working from a modest, temporary space. While it's smart to be prepared, be wary of getting too much insurance. The last thing you want is to spend precious money on services that you don't actually require.

Insurance can be complicated, so you may wish to consult an insurance broker to help determine exactly what it is you need. He might even be aware of certain tailored packages that already exist for your specific industry. Whether you seek professional help or move forward on your own, be sure that your business has enough of the coverage it needs to withstand any foreseeable conflict—and perhaps some of the less foreseeable ones as well. Even the smallest of accidents or oversights can potentially wipe out your business if you're not sufficiently protected.

TANK TIP

"Don't take shortcuts when it comes to the logistical and operation stuff. So many people try to do everything themselves to save money. But in the long run you'll only end up losing money that way."

—TRAVIS PERRY, FOUNDER OF CHORDBUDDY

PATENTS: A PRIMER

If you decide to patent your idea or product, there are three different types of patents you can pursue, each with its own specifications:

Utility patent: Making up more than 90 percent of patents, the utility patent is issued for the invention of "a new and useful process, machine, manufacture, or composition of matter, or a new and useful improvement thereof," according to the U.S. Patent and Trademark Office (PTO). This patent protects a product for up to twenty years and carries with it regular maintenance fees.

Design patent: Issued for "a new, original, and ornamental design for an article of manufacture," the design patent will protect your product or idea for fourteen years and carries no applicable maintenance fees.

Plant patent: The least popular of the three, the plant patent protects "a new and distinct, invented or discovered asexually reproduced plant including cultivated sports, mutants, hybrids, and newly found seedlings, other than a tuber propagated plant or plant found in an uncultivated state." A plant patent is valid for twenty years and carries no applicable maintenance fees.

MOSHE WEISS, SOUNDBENDER (SEASON 4)

BIG IDEA: A magnetic, power-free iPad amplifier that improves sound quality and clarity.

INVESTOR: Daymond John

Like many entrepreneurs, Rabbi Moshe Weiss has always been remarkably curious. Working in his parents' bakery as a child, he was exposed to business at an early age. As he grew, so too did his interests. Eventually he found himself working in the education sector. But when the school he helped found was forced to close its doors, Moshe felt deflated and uncertain of the next move.

To help lift his spirits, a donor to the school, now one of Moshe's good friends, presented him with a gift: an iPad 2.

"It was very thoughtful," Moshe recalls. "After only using it for a few days, I realized the quality of the speakers weren't very good, so I got a Band-Aid box and propped it up to bend the sound."

The contraption worked, so Moshe began looking online for a product that would do the same thing. But, shockingly, he couldn't find any such product. Was it possible? Nobody had thought to create such a thing? Moshe paused for a moment in silence. "This is it," he thought. "This is my salvation." And right then and there the SoundBender journey began.

To get the product to market, Moshe borrowed seed money from a friend. Thanks to a few family connections, he was also able to hire a patent attorney and gain access to other important resources at little to no cost. "It was tough," he says. "I really was starting from scratch."

Once the product was designed, Moshe launched a Kickstarter campaign to raise additional financing. It proved to be a success. From the $10,000 the campaign brought in, Moshe was able to make his molds and begin selling his product.

Almost one year later, Moshe stood backstage, preparing to present his product in the tank. Not only was he committed to proving himself to the Sharks, he knew he'd have to prove himself to the world.

"The way I looked at it, I wasn't just pitching to the Sharks," says Moshe. "I was pitching to my consumer and to the entire business community. I wanted a deal, of course, but I knew there was more to it than that."

Clearly this was a solid approach, because Moshe scored a deal with Daymond John.

"Not only did being on *Shark Tank* boost my sales," says Moshe, "it took about six years off the business-building process. Overnight I gained the credibility I needed to take my business to the next level."

In many ways, Moshe's business has been a community effort. Without the help of friends and family, Kickstarter supporters, *Shark Tank* fans, and of course Daymond John, the idea for SoundBender might never have advanced past the Band-Aid box.

"So many entrepreneurs make the mistake of thinking they know everything about everything. But my approach has always been to surround myself with people whom I trust and who have my best interests at heart. That's how you become successful."

   To find out more about SoundBender, visit The SoundBender. com or follow them on Twitter @SoundBenderTM.

REAL-WORLD WISDOM: "Work with people who complement your strengths. I have ADHD. I'm like a kite ready to fly up into the sky. And any kite knows that to be successful they need a good anchor. So I choose to only work with very grounded people who can help me keep the business anchored."

PART THREE
MONEY MATTERS

KEVIN O'LEARY

CLAIM TO FAME: Business tycoon who turned a $10,000 loan into a software business worth $4.2 billion.

THE WAY I WORK: "I view my money as an army that I send out to do war every day. I expect it to kill the enemy and bring home the dead bodies, which will increase my net worth."

THE ART OF SUCCESS

Growing up, I wanted to be a photographer, but my father pointed out that it was going to be a very difficult way to make a living. Of course he was right, and ultimately I chose to go down a different professional path. But I believe being a great businessperson is half about being a great artist.

Today I'm still an avid photographer, and I can afford to buy the best equipment and travel the world taking images. In fact, I have my very first exhibit next month. And the only reason I can do any of this is because I've chosen a career that allows for it. That's what being an entrepreneur is all about: achieving financial freedom.

If you're going to be an entrepreneur, you must understand one thing: business is war. It's black or white; there's no gray. You're either making money or you're losing it. Admitting that truth can sometimes be politically embarrassing, but it's the only reason ever to go into business. You also must understand that it's a process—a tide that goes in and out. I've lost millions, and I've made millions. What's important is that at the end of it all you come out on top—that you're able to provide for your family and do with your time what you wish.

I've waited my whole life to be a photographer, and the only reason I can do it today is because I've achieved financial freedom. It's really the American Dream.

Step one is to decide which accounting method you'll use to track your financial progress: cash or accrual. While the cash method is the more utilized choice, certain operations may be served better by using the accrual method.

Cash: Under the cash method, revenue isn't recorded until the cash is actually received. Similarly, expenses aren't accounted for until they are actually paid. EXAMPLE: You run a small janitorial business and signed on a new corporate client in March. You give them ninety days to pay their invoice and you deposit the check in June. Under this method, the revenue would be recorded in June, not March.

Accrual: Under the accrual method, revenue is recorded when the order occurs or the service is provided, not when the payment is actually received. Likewise, using this method, expenses are accounted for when they are incurred, not when they are paid. EXAMPLE: You purchase a new copy machine in July and have six months to pay the manufacturer. Even if you don't pay the bill until January of the following year, under this method you would record the expense in July.

After learning more about each method, it's easy to understand why most small businesses prefer the cash method: it gives a real-time picture of the company's finances and allows them to see how much money they actually have available. However, by providing a more accurate long-term projection, the accrual method can be a better choice for certain types of organizations. What's more, if your business has sales over $5 million per year or sells inventory to the public (with sales grossing over $1 million per year), you don't have a say in the matter; you are legally required to use the accrual method.

Make sure to consider how your chosen accounting method will affect your business at tax time. If you're using the accrual method, for instance, the expenses you incur in one year may not be deductible until the following, depending on when the payment was actually made. Let's use the copy machine example from above. Although you ordered the machine in July 2012, you didn't actually pay the invoice until January 2013. Therefore, under the accrual method you would declare the deduction in the latter year instead of the former, even though you recorded the expense in your own accounting in the first year.

Once you've chosen your preferred accounting method, the next step is to develop a solid financial management process. If you're a new entrepreneur and not familiar with basic accounting principles, just the phrase "financial management process" may be enough to send you rushing off to the next chapter. Don't let it! While accounting can be overwhelming at first, it's a vital part of being a responsible business owner and can often be the difference between success and failure. From anticipating pitfalls to projecting growth, a strong financial management process is essential to the overall sustainability of your business. Here are a few tasks every business should practice:

Keep receipts and invoices: You'll want to get in the habit of keeping exceptional records right from the start. This includes everything from collecting expense receipts to tracking supplier and client invoices. For some businesses, this might be a daily task—think retail—while others might only need to do it every few weeks. While the record-keeping process ranges greatly in time and complexity, for many companies it shouldn't take more than a few minutes each day.

Record information: A filing cabinet full of crumpled receipts and invoices won't do you much good. If you've taken the time to save records, you might as well devote some additional energy to organizing and entering them in a centralized database.

Before the rise of technology, many business owners managed their books by hand in a ledger. Today, there is a wide variety of software, apps, and online tools that help companies track and organize records efficiently. While very small operations may be able to manage their bookkeeping process on a standard spreadsheet, most businesses will require specialized software or online tools, like QuickBooks or FreshBooks. Whatever program you use, be sure to enter your income and expenses regularly and thoroughly. You'll need all of that information to run proper financial statements.

Produce financial statements: Preparing and reviewing financial statements is pivotal to the long-term health of your business. Luckily, creating these necessary reports is simple if you're keeping accurate records and recording them with basic bookkeeping software. Financial statements are valuable because they provide you with a real-time snapshot of how your company is performing. Moreover, they answer important questions like: Are you generating enough income to cover your expenses? Is that income coming in fast enough to pay your bills on time? Is your company growing from month to month? For a new business owner these questions are crucial, especially during the startup phase. Depending on your chosen bookkeeping software, you will have access to a variety of different financial statements at the push of a button, but here are the three you should run on a regular basis:

Profit and loss statement: Commonly referred to as a P&L, this vital income statement does exactly what it sounds like: tracks how much profit or loss your business has experienced over a specified period of time, be that a week, month, or year. It also allows you to see your net income and, depending on your accounting software's capabilities, which products or services are performing better—and where you're overspending. Most businesses choose to run a P&L report on a weekly or monthly basis.

Balance sheet: This report provides a snapshot of your company's overall financial position. In essence, it tells you what you *own* and what you *owe*, allowing you to see an accurate picture of your assets and liabilities. It's this statement that also reveals your net worth (also referred to as "net value" or "equity"). This is a critical document when trying to secure an investment or loan. If you're a regular *Shark Tank* viewer, then you already know how important this document is to your business. Without a balance sheet, an entrepreneur would never be able to identify her company's actual worth, thus providing no accurate basis for a valuation.

Cash flow statement: Running a business can be expensive. The cash flow statement allows you to see how much cash you're bringing in at any given moment and tells you whether you have enough money to cover your expenses. Because, as it turns out, even profitable companies are not always able to pay their bills on time. Let's say, for instance, that you've brought in $100,000 of new business from four customers who have been given ninety days to pay their invoice. At the same time, however, you are required to pay *your* bills within thirty days. Even though your business is making a profit, you'll still struggle to cover your bills each month if the cash is taking ninety days to actually come in-house. The cash flow statement allows you to identify this information in advance, so you can plan appropriately.

If you have little to no experience with accounting, this probably seems like a lot of information. In fact, it may be helpful to read this section over a couple times. While you will most likely hire an accountant or bookkeeper at some point,

"Cash is the lifeblood of your business. There are very few things in business that will kill you, but running out of cash is one of those things. You can recover from almost any other mistake, but if you run out of cash you're dead. You don't need to be an accountant, but if you don't know your numbers you can't run a business. It's that simple."

ROBERT

as the founder it's your responsibility to have, at the very least, a basic understanding of accounting principles.

PREPARING FOR TAXES

Survey a hundred entrepreneurs on their favorite part of running a business, and you're likely to hear a range of inspired answers. From the excitement of tackling daily challenges to the pride that comes with financial independence, owning a business has plenty of perks. But one thing you probably won't hear an entrepreneur rave about is paying taxes.

As the saying goes, "Nothing is certain but death and taxes," and for the small business owner this couldn't be more accurate. Without fail, each year the federal and local government will come knocking on your door in search of their piece of the pie. From individual and corporate income to payroll and sales, you can rest assured that anything that can be taxed will be taxed.

Of course the best way to grow your income without owing the government an arm and a leg is to claim legitimate deductions from your business expenses. But it's not always as easy as it sounds. Most people are under the false impression that once you become a business owner, pretty much every expense is tax-deductible. Unfortunately it's a little more complicated than that.

According to the IRS, only "ordinary and necessary" expenses can be deducted from your business income, including such things as supplies, insurance, rent, and equipment. While you can also deduct items like entertainment, travel, and vehicle expenses, those fall under different rules, and are often only partially deductible.

While calculating your deductions, there are two primary types of expenses to understand: current and capital. Current expenses are incurred on a daily basis and can include everything from rent to travel. Capital expenses, also referred to as "business assets," are generally larger purchases that have a life of at least one year. This type of expense cannot be fully deducted in the year it occurs, and instead must be spread out over the life of the object. Let's say, for instance, that you purchased a piece of machinery for your T-shirt business. Because that equipment would be used over the course of many years, it would be considered a capital expense.

Deductions are vital to the prosperity of your business and should be recorded accurately and honestly. If you've been diligent with your accounting throughout the year, this should be a fairly manageable process.

Once you've figured out your deductions, it's time to sit down and tally up how much you'll owe. Depending on your location, incorporation structure, and type of business, you will likely be subject to three different types of taxes: federal, state, and city or county. There are a number of factors that affect your specific tax requirements, so it's best to consult with the appropriate government agencies. Below, however, you'll find a generalized breakdown of the types of taxes you can expect to pay:

Sole proprietors: As you learned in the previous chapter, under this legal structure, income from your business is treated as personal income. Along with the standard form 1040, which shows how much money you've earned, you must also declare your company's profit on a Schedule C and pay self-employment taxes, which is reported on Schedule SE. Currently, the self-employment tax rate is 15.3 percent, which goes toward Social Security and Medicare.

Partnerships: Similar to sole proprietors, partners are taxed, not the partnership itself. That said, partnerships still must report income and losses each year. While partnerships must also pay income and self-employment taxes, a partner can deduct half of the self-employment tax at the end of the year.

LLCs: Just as with sole proprietors and partnerships, under an LLC, income is taxed to the owner, not the business itself. While you must pay self-employment tax under an LLC, you need only report income and losses to the IRS if you have more than two members. Although the IRS does not tax LLCs, certain states may require additional taxes to be paid, which can range in size. Most LLCs can incorporate in any state, so it may be in your best interest to explore options outside of your current home state. Similar to how many corporations choose to incorporate in Delaware, many small businesses prefer Wyoming and Nevada for tax and protection reasons.

Although nobody likes paying taxes, it's crucial that you keep track of how much you'll owe and prepare accordingly. There's nothing worse than thinking you've made a profit only to find out that you've miscalculated your tax obligations.

Keep in mind, businesses that expect to owe the IRS more than $1,000 are required to pay estimated taxes on a quarterly basis. Assuming your tax rate is somewhere between 25 and 33 percent, if you plan on making more than about

SHARK BITE

"Taxation only occurs after profits have been made. So worrying about taxes is always a good thing, because it means you're making money. I would love to have that problem with many of my investments."

KEVIN

$3,000 in adjusted gross income over the course of the year, you should be paying quarterly taxes. Of course if you end up paying more than you owe, you'll get a refund for that amount at the end of the year.

Even though estimated quarterly taxes are required for many businesses, very often new business owners can't afford to sacrifice the capital up front and would rather pay all of their taxes at the end of the year. Be aware that if you choose to go this route, you'll be subject to penalty fees that can range in size and complexity. What's more, if you don't pay quarterly taxes, it's even more imperative to stay on top of your accounting, or you could be stuck with a huge tax bill at the end of the year.

Although any person or business owner can prepare his own taxes, it's worth spending the extra bit of money to hire an accountant. Tax preparation can be confusing, and even a small mistake can end up costing you big. If you're starting a corporation, as opposed to a sole proprietorship, partnership, or LLC, you should most definitely seek professional assistance. The process is far too complicated to handle on your own.

DON'T MIX BUSINESS AND PLEASURE: KEEPING A BUSINESS CHECKING ACCOUNT

No matter the size of your company, you should always keep your business and personal finances separate, which means you'll need to open a business checking account. The process of setting up a business checking account varies slightly based on your location and incorporation status. However, there are a few key things to consider when shopping for a good one:

Past, present, future: If you already have a relationship with a bank, you may find it most convenient to open a separate business checking account at that institution. But it also doesn't hurt to shop around and see what the competition has to offer. While you must be realistic about your current financial needs, you should also be looking ahead to the future. Will you need to eventually secure a business loan or additional line of credit? Will this bank help your business grow? Would you rather choose a large corporate institution or a smaller, local establishment? These are all important questions.

Fees and penalties: The fees for personal and business checking vary greatly, even at the same bank. Will you be charged for online banking? Does the bank require a minimum balance? If so, how much? And what will happen if you fall below it? Be vigilant with your banker about getting all the necessary information regarding fees and penalties before signing up. As it turns out, free checking isn't always free.

Online banking: Banks are no longer just brick-and-mortar operations. Over the last decade, a slew of high-quality Internet banks (or "direct banks") have popped up online, many with very competitive offerings. Once you've assessed your financial needs, you may wish to explore the option of using an Internet bank.

8

UNDERSTANDING FINANCING

I t happens all the time: An ambitious entrepreneur comes up with a brilliant idea and decides to start a company. The first couple months seem to go off without a hitch. Sure, there are long days and the occasional roadblock, but all in all, it's smooth sailing. And then things slowly start to break down. All of a sudden there seems to be a never-ending flood of unforeseen challenges that eat up precious time and resources. Before long, everything is off-schedule and money is tight. And then it happens: that brutal moment of clarity. The business is quickly running out of funds, and unless more capital can be immediately secured, it doesn't stand a chance of surviving.

This type of situation occurs more often than you might imagine. In fact, some of the best ideas are never executed, or only half-executed, due to a lack of financial planning. Enthusiasm and optimism are wonderful traits for the entrepreneur to possess, but only when coupled with equal parts wisdom and foresight.

Starting a business, any business, requires capital, money, cash. Some companies will need an abundance of it, while others can get by on the bare minimum. No matter how much funding your particular business may require, it's a good idea to have a basic sense of your startup costs prior to launching. Otherwise, you could end up out of business or, worse, bankrupt.

To accurately assess the cost of starting your company, you should consider the whole financial picture. Unfortunately, there isn't a standard formula for determining expenses, as variables shift depending on location, incorporation status, and business type. There are, however, a few expenses that most business owners can anticipate:

Inventory: This includes things like raw materials, shipping, packaging, and other expenses related to inventory. If applicable, make sure to also factor in things like shipping insurance, sales commissions, and any warehouse expenses you may incur. Most likely, the majority of these costs will be ongoing throughout the life of your business.

Professional services: Setting up the legal structure of your business, hiring an accountant or lawyer, acquiring trademarks or patents—all of these should be integrated into the cost of your professional services. This category also includes items like permits and licenses and the hiring of additional outside consultants.

Sales and marketing: Business cards, stationery, and other general marketing materials are all examples of expenses you should include in your sales and marketing budget. Eventually you'll need to set up a website, advertise your products or services, and attend industry-related conferences or trade shows. Everything that has to do with marketing or lead generation should be budgeted under this category.

Operational costs: These can include anything from insurance to utilities. When factoring in your operational costs, make sure not to overlook expenses like rent, furniture, Internet, parking, office supplies, and other administrative needs your company may have.

Infrastructure: Depending on your type of business, you may require certain types of machinery, equipment, or other costly pieces of infrastructure. Almost every business will need to purchase computers and various other pieces of technology. Do some basic research to find out how much you should expect to pay for items related to basic business infrastructure, and make sure to account for it in your budget.

When calculating your startup costs, you'll want to make sure to differentiate the onetime expenses from ongoing costs. Incorporating your business and acquiring the necessary equipment, for instance, are onetime costs, while inventory and rent are ongoing expenses. Therefore, if you're putting together a six-month budget, you'll need to factor in the ongoing expenses appropriately.

If you're struggling to figure out exactly how much money you'll need to start, you may find it helpful to talk to somebody who has experience launching a similar type of business. While your local competition probably won't be willing to share information about their costs, it's likely you can find someone just slightly outside your industry to help. Of course there are plenty of online resources to get you on track as

SHARK BITE

"When it comes to startup costs, there are always going to be surprises because you're on a new journey. Often, first-time entrepreneurs think everyone will love their idea, so they jump right in and risk a lot of money. You've got to be realistic. You don't want to end up with a warehouse full of product that nobody's buying."

LORI

well, some of which you can find listed in the Tools and Resources section in the back of the book.

If you've ever started a business before, you know how easy it is to go over budget. In fact, general wisdom says you should double or triple the original number you come up with, given that even the most prepared business owner can't anticipate every expense. Begin calculating your budget, and make sure you've included all the categories above. The last thing you want is a large, unaccounted-for expense throwing you off budget.

FINANCING YOUR BUSINESS

Now that you've assessed your startup costs, you may have realized it's going to cost a lot more money to start your company than you initially thought. That doesn't have to be a deal-breaker. Whether you're starting a small home business or a more complicated operation, there are plenty of ways to secure capital, each with its own implications.

When it comes to financing your business, it's less a matter of right-or-wrong choices and more a matter of which method is more suitable for your particular situation. Before you decide which financing method is right for you, you must first understand your options:

Self-funding: Your first option is to self-fund the business and take no outside capital. Some of the most successful entrepreneurs in the world have started companies by self-funding—some even prefer it. The primary benefit of not taking an outside investment is that you remain in full control of the business. There's only one cook in the kitchen, and it's you! Of course self-funding also comes with the most personal risk. Investing all your savings into a business, for instance, means you could potentially lose it all if the business fails. While many small business owners start by self-funding their company, most will eventually seek some type of outside financing.

Friends and family: After self-funding, the next most viable option is to approach friends and family for capital. This can be touchy, mainly because it has the potential to go either way. On the one hand, if the business succeeds, you have the opportunity to make the people closest to you a nice return. But on the other hand, if the business fails, those same people could lose their entire investment.

Before reaching out to friends and family, you must first decide how you wish to structure the deal: as equity or debt. An equity investor becomes part-owner in the company and shares in all the profits. In a debt transaction, the lender becomes a creditor to the entrepreneur and is repaid based on the terms of the agreement. Decide which structure is best for you and your business *before* reaching out to your friends and family for a potential investment.

Crowdfunding: The newest and most popular type of fundraising, crowdfunding is a collective method of raising capital in which a large group of people pool their money together to fund a single project or business. Almost always fueled by technology, crowdfunding has become one of the very best methods of raising capital, especially in the tech sector. When crowdfunding a project, investors do not typically receive equity or repayment. Instead, they're offered a variety of incentives based on their respective investment level. If you were raising money to start a pretzel business, for instance, participants might receive a box of your first batch or get the opportunity to name one of the products.

"Crowdfunding is something every entrepreneur should look into, no matter what type of business they're starting," says Barbara Corcoran. "It's the new frontier of financing."

Although crowdfunding is relatively new, it can be incredibly effective. In fact, some companies have raised millions of dollars using platforms like Kickstarter and Indiegogo.

Angel investment: After dipping into your personal funds and the funds of those in your network, you may find you need help from an angel investor or venture capitalist. An angel investor is typically a wealthy individual who uses her own money to invest in a company. While an angel investor may provide less funding than a venture capitalist, he also demands less control. Most angels, for instance, do not require a seat on your board (if you even have a board) and carry out a much shorter and simpler diligence process. By and large, angel investors tend to be more flexible than venture capitalists, but also less able or willing to give very large sums of money (i.e., over $1 million). In exchange for their funds, angels typically seek equity ownership or convertible debt—debt that can be converted into equity at a later point in the future. When the Sharks invest in companies in the tank they're acting as angel investors.

Venture capital: If you have a high-risk, high-potential company that needs large amounts of money, venture capital may be the right choice for you. These days, venture capitalists most often invest in technology companies with an assumed high rate of return (think 25 percent or more).

Ranging from investments of $1 million to $5 million and up, venture capitalists seek equity in the companies they fund, as opposed to debt. From seed funding to taking a company public, there are six stages of venture capital funding that are designed to help a business throughout every stage of its development. While you should understand the role of venture capital, most first-time business owners will not require this type of funding.

SHARK BITE

"You have a much better shot of surviving with your own money than with the next guy's money, because it means so much more to you and makes every mistake so much more painful. It's the only way to learn what you really have and how far you can stretch each dollar."

BARBARA

Although some entrepreneurs may be able to get by self-funding their business or taking small investments from friends and family, others will require a much larger investment. No matter how much capital you need, it's important to know how to sell your business to investors. In other words, you've got to learn how to pitch.

MASTERING THE PITCH

When it comes to pitching your business, the more prepared you can be the better. Just think about some of the entrepreneurs you've seen on *Shark Tank*. In almost every instance, it's the most prepared, knowledgeable business owner who gets a deal. The good news is that if you've been following along with this book, you've already done a lot of the work. But before you can approach an investor, you must identify what you should present and how you should present it.

It may sound obvious, but the first step is to understand your business inside and out and know how to communicate it in a straightforward way. You must also be able to explain your business model in an equally concise manner. In under two minutes, the investor should understand what exactly you're selling and how you plan to make money. In theory this may sound simple, but many entrepreneurs find it difficult to summarize their business. Test yourself by attempting to explain your business to a stranger in less than 120 seconds. You may be surprised at how challenging this exercise can be.

But remember, a successful pitch is about more than just communicating the business model. The investor must believe in more than just your product or service; she must believe in your ability to sell it. So you'll want to demonstrate a clear understanding of your industry and target market from the start. Being able to identify competitors and trends within your market will only help gain the investor's trust.

In the previous chapter you learned how crucial it is to know your numbers, and that's especially true when it comes to pitching. Even if you don't consider yourself a "numbers person," a potential investor will want to know that you have a sound grip on your company's financials. Don't forget, if you do score a deal, you'll be playing ball with the investor's money. He'll want to make sure you know the game.

And finally, you should have a reasonable idea of where your business is headed. Investors don't expect you to walk in the door with a wildly successful, hugely profitable company. If that was the case why would you be there in the first place? What they want to see is that you have a sound and realistic plan to grow the business. Anyone can start a company; what they're looking for is vision and your ability to execute. Only once you feel like you have these necessary pieces of information in place should you think about pitching.

When it comes time to pitch your business, your information and presentation should be seamless and polished. Here are a few ways to create a better pitch:

Know your audience: Who exactly are you pitching to? Are you speaking with a large investment firm or with a single angel investor? Maybe you're pitching to a good family friend. While every pitch can have the same basic information, the presentation should be tailored to the audience receiving it.

Start off strong: Investors hear pitches all the time, and you don't want to lose them before you've even begun. Craft an opener that's compelling enough to grab their attention from the start.

Keep it simple: Just because the investor may understand *business* doesn't mean she will necessarily understand *your* business. Avoid using a lot of industry jargon or making the business appear too complicated. A simple and concise pitch will serve you better than one that's confusing or convoluted.

Tell a story: While it's important to stay focused, you don't want your pitch to be dry. Tell a compelling story about the problem you're trying to solve and the market opportunity you wish to seize. Data is vital and you should be able to back up your idea. But don't underestimate the benefit of storytelling.

Humanize the experience: You started this business for a reason, right? If you believe in what you're doing—and you should—let that passion come through in your pitch. If you're funny, be funny. If you're excited, be excited (to a degree). Yes, you should be professional, but don't be afraid to also be human. Remember, this is a partnership, and the investor is interested in getting to know you as much as he is interested in getting to know your business.

Avoid exaggeration: If your company grossed $150,000 last year and you're projecting $20 million next year, you better be able to back up that forecast with data. It's easy to rely on exaggeration and hyperbole when trying to impress an investor, but be wary of going down that path. Nobody wants to work with someone who's out of touch. Optimism is encouraged, but only if it's grounded in reality.

Stay on your game: There are a hundred different things that can go wrong during a pitch: your slides don't work, you forget an important piece of data, the investor loses interest. If something happens and you need to take a second to regroup, take it, but don't let a hiccup ruin the entire pitch.

Be ready for questions: After your pitch is over, the investor will most likely have a handful of follow-up questions. This is where all that knowledge about your target market, competition, and financials really comes in handy. Prepare yourself for as many different types of questions as you can. Rest assured that if there's something about your business you're trying to hide, the investor will eventually uncover it. It's better to be uncertain than dishonest.

Practice, practice, practice: While the greatest pitches may appear smooth and effortless, you can bet that plenty of work goes into their preparation. In fact, the most seamless pitches are usually the ones that require the most practice. Devote as much time as you need to fine-tuning your pitch. Practice in front of a mirror; practice in front of friends; practice in front of strangers if they'll let you. The more work you put into the preparation, the more likely you'll be to secure an investment.

SHARK BITE

"The best pitch isn't a pitch. It's an honest presentation of what you are going to do, how you are going to get there, and why it matters."

MARK

USING YOUR PERSONAL CREDIT CARD: A WARNING

How many times have you heard this story: An entrepreneur has a great idea and decides to start a company. Unable to receive funding from the bank or outside investors, the newly minted business owner bootstraps his way to success by using personal credit cards to launch the venture. And then, just as he's maxed out his last card, the business takes off and his investment is paid back. Sound familiar?

Statistics cited by the U.S. Small Business Administration show that over 65 percent of all business owners use credit for business purchases. But here's the scary part: only 50 percent of that is business credit—the rest is personal.

Securing a line of business credit isn't as easy as it once was, especially if your business has yet to bring in any money. And while personal credit cards can most certainly help an entrepreneur build a business—even the founders of Google initially funded their company with credit cards—you must understand the seriousness of using personal credit to fund your business.

Assuming you've incorporated as either an LLC or corporation, your personal finances are subject to a certain level of protection. However, if you use personal funds to finance your business, and that business fails, you are left with the debt. What's more, a credit card company can choose to reduce your credit limit at any point, potentially eliminating your primary source of funding.

You should only use credit cards as a financing tool if you feel as though you're responsible enough to make regular payments and willing to take the risk. And be sure to keep spectacular records, so you can legitimately and thoroughly reimburse yourself when the business begins making money. Because here's the thing: the story about the entrepreneur starting her company with the credit card isn't a myth. It's only the last part where things get dicey: the happy ending.

JIM TSELIKIS AND SABIN LOMAC, COUSINS MAINE LOBSTER (SEASON 4)

BIG IDEA: Fresh Maine lobster available through an LA-based food truck or delivered nationwide.
INVESTOR: Barbara Corcoran

When Cousins Maine Lobster founders Jim Tselikis and Sabin Lomac walked into the tank, they'd only been in business for three months. But you never would have known it from watching their pitch. Determined to land a deal, the food truck owners came up with a plan: in the weeks leading up to the taping, Jim and Sabin rewatched all the previous seasons of *Shark Tank* and wrote down every question that had ever been asked. Working together, they prepared two answers for each possible question. The result of all their hard work was a deal with Barbara Corcoran.

"These guys are perfect role models for other entrepreneurs," says Barbara. "It's not just about having a great pitch. The people who walk away with a deal are the ones who are the most prepared."

Preparation is nothing new for Jim and Sabin. When the cousins first started their company, they were met with an immediate challenge: they lived on different coasts. Not only did the lobster-flinging duo have day jobs to consider, they had to compete with a taxing three-hour time difference.

"It may not sound like a lot, but it was," says Sabin. "Working a day job and starting a company is hard enough without your business partner living three thousand miles away."

But location wasn't the only challenge Jim and Sabin faced. This was their first time starting a company together, so they had to learn how to transform their relationship from one of family members to one of business partners.

"Before we got into this, we had to assess everything," recalls Jim. "There are so many issues that can come up when running a business. We didn't want anything to tarnish our relationship as family."

So the cousins decided to do what they do best: prepare. Before starting the company, Jim and Sabin took a series of personality and behavioral assessment tests to discover more about how they'd work as a team.

Among many things, the tests revealed that Jim and Sabin handle conflict very differently. Jim prefers to push through a challenge, while Sabin is more apt to find creative ways to get around it. Those insights have played a crucial role in how they've run the business.

"Knowing those things from the beginning took away some of the day-to-day surprises that come with running a company," says Jim. "Business is like a marriage. The more you know about your partner, the better it will be."

So how is Cousins Maine Lobster doing today? After appearing on the show and making a deal with Barbara, the company experienced incredible growth. Between launching another food truck, opening a pop-up restaurant, and running a busy e-commerce store, Jim and Sabin have found tremendous success—and they've only been in a business for one year.

"There are still a lot of things that Jim and I don't know," says Sabin. "Some people are too vain to admit it, but we're very open and honest. We've always been very eager and prepared to learn. We've had to be."

To find out more about Cousins Maine Lobster, visit Cousins MaineLobster.com or follow them on Twitter @CMLobster.

REAL-WORLD WISDOM: "You have to know everything about your particular business. A lot of people are too proud to admit when they don't know something, so they decide to ignore it instead of actually learning. That never works. As an entrepreneur you need to be hyper-curious about your business and your industry."

PART FOUR
OPEN FOR BUSINESS

DAYMOND JOHN

CLAIM TO FAME: Fashion mogul and branding expert who founded the globally recognized fashion brand FUBU.

THE WAY I WORK: "I invest in people. My leadership style is to give employees full responsibility for their jobs and create a benefit system that allows them to feel personally connected to the results."

THE 100TH ROAD

I believe you're either born thinking like an entrepreneur or you're not. It's that simple. You either have that special thing or you don't.

I don't have a traditional business background. I did it the hard way. When I first started selling shirts, I had to literally get up in people's faces with the product. Social media didn't exist yet. I wasn't able to put my product on a global platform and see how many people liked it or objected to it. I had to actually go out there and do it. So that's what I did. I'd try a hundred different roads, and if ninety-nine didn't work then I'd go with number one hundred.

Even though I learned as I went, there was one thing I did know from the start: nobody was going to get up before me or go to bed after me. Nobody could outwork me. And that's because I loved my product. I believed in it. And that's the most important part of being an entrepreneur. You've got to love what you do. You must absolutely be obsessed with your business—every single day. And you've got to love your customers too; because that's the only way they'll ever love you back.

Look, there isn't just one path to achieve success. You've got to figure that out on your own, and that means staying true to yourself. Not only because it's important for you personally, but because it's important for your business. The easiest thing to sell is the truth, especially in an age where transparency rules.

Being on *Shark Tank* has opened my eyes. It's taught me that I may not always be able to spot the next Pet Rock or Snuggie. It's showed me that there are some amazing little ideas that have the power to become really big ideas. But most of all, *Shark Tank* has taught me that there is more innovation out there than I ever knew existed. It's not about big business. It's about small business. It's about the entrepreneur.

9

UP AND RUNNING

Opening for business can be the most thrilling part of an entrepreneur's journey. Whether you've been dreaming about this day for months or years, launching a business is always an electrifying experience. But before you introduce the world to your great idea, you must be certain that you are physically, mentally, and emotionally ready for the wild adventure that lies ahead.

Running a business, especially during the first year, requires tremendous focus and energy. Once you say, "go," it's difficult to turn back, so it's critical that you're as prepared as possible.

"The standard rule of thumb is that you're going to sell half as much as you think you are and your costs are going to be twice as high," says Robert Herjavec. "You're not going to hit a lot of success in your first year, so you've got to prepare for some degree of failure."

Below you'll find a checklist that will help ensure you've taken all the major steps toward opening your business. Comb through the list and make sure you can check off each item. With all the twists and turns you're bound to encounter along the way, your goal should be to minimize the unknowns. This may very well be the last opportunity to pause and reflect before launching your business.

BUSINESS PREP CHECKLIST

☐ Identified your strengths and weaknesses
☐ Assessed your lifestyle and made any necessary changes
☐ Evaluated your idea and zeroed in on the specific problem you're trying to solve
☐ Discovered your target market
☐ Researched your competition
☐ Weighed the pros and cons of starting a business versus buying one
☐ Chosen a name for your business
☐ Developed a value proposition
☐ Created a mission statement and began considering core values
☐ Developed a solid business model
☐ Created a pricing strategy
☐ Written some type of business plan
☐ Incorporated your business
☐ Secured any patents, trademarks, or copyrights
☐ Acquired any outside legal or accounting assistance
☐ Purchased the necessary insurance
☐ Developed a system for managing your financial books
☐ Began tracking and recording your expenses
☐ Educated yourself on your various tax responsibilities
☐ Opened a business checking account
☐ Assessed your basic startup costs

SHARK BITE

"My favorite saying is 'We always overestimate what we can achieve in one year and underestimate what we can achieve in ten.' When I started my current business ten years ago, we thought we'd sell $5 million in the first year; we sold $400,000. It took us five years to get to $6 million in sales, but in the next five, we got to $155 million. We were way overconfident when thinking about our first year, and not confident enough when planning the next ten."

ROBERT

☐ Budgeted for at least the first year
☐ Crafted a strong and compelling pitch
☐ Secured any necessary outside financing

If after reading the list above you feel calm and confident, you may be ready to launch. Only one question still remains: Are you prepared operationally?

While some ventures take time to grow, others experience a burst of interest from the start. If you're lucky enough to be in the latter category, you'll want to be certain that you're able to deliver. Otherwise, you may be unable to capitalize on the initial buzz. Unless you have a very small service-based company where everything is run in-house, you'll need to start developing a reliable network of trusted vendors.

CHOOSING THE RIGHT VENDOR

While the word "vendor" can have multiple meanings, in this book it refers to any outside company that provides services to your business, including suppliers and manufacturers. If you have a granola company, for instance, your vendors might include the supplier of the ingredients, the manufacturing plant, the fulfillment center, and any other company that plays a role in the development, creation, or distribution of your product.

Remember, your vendors are a reflection of both you and your brand, so it's critical that you only work with the very best you can afford. While each business will have its own specific needs, there are a few characteristics that every business owner should look for in a vendor:

Quality: You can have the most beautiful store in the world, the greatest customer service, and the best management in the business, but if your product is bad, your product is bad. End of story. Skimping on quality for the sake of better margins is not only ethically questionable, it's shortsighted as well. Most companies offer some sort of return policy. If your product is poor, you better believe your customers will want their money back, and a high volume of returns can throw a business terribly off track.

From engineering to production, quality is key, and that starts with your vendor. Be sure to ask specific questions about their commitment to quality. Depending on your particular business, you may wish to make a site visit and evaluate the company yourself.

Reliability: Diane Sawyer once said, "Great questions make great reporting." For the entrepreneur, great questions make great business. And this couldn't be more true than when it comes to choosing vendors. Ask questions—lots of them. In fact, if you don't feel at least a little embarrassed by how many questions you're asking, you probably should be asking more.

It's imperative that your vendors demonstrate the utmost reliability and dependability. If they break promises to you, you'll be forced to break promises to your customers—and that can ruin your company's reputation. Find out about their history, what their capacity is like, and how many other clients they're working with. Do they have enough inventory in stock to fulfill your orders in a timely manner? Is their organization run well? Don't be afraid to ask for a list of references. The findings you uncover will play a critical role in your decision.

Pricing: The more it costs to produce a product, the less profit you'll end up making. Therefore it's essential to choose a vendor who can offer competitive pricing. But don't just go with the lowest bid. You know what they say: if it seems too good to be true, it probably is. For instance, if one vendor gives you a quote that's 50 percent lower than the rest, you'll want to make sure you know exactly why they're able to offer such a low price. Are they underpaying workers? Skimping on quality? While you want to get the best deal possible, it's never worth working with a vendor who regularly cuts corners just to save a couple bucks.

Payment options: As you learned in Chapter Seven, cash is king. When choosing a vendor, it's important to fully understand their specific payment terms. Will you be responsible for issuing payment when an order is placed, or will you have a certain period of time to settle the invoice? And if it's the latter, exactly what kind of allotment will you have? The more time you have to pay a vendor, the more time you have to bring money into the business. Be sure to understand the terms before signing any agreement.

Service: It's guaranteed that at some point there will be a miscommunication or misunderstanding between you and your vendor. That's just part of doing business. So it's always a good idea to choose a vendor who is service-minded and committed to supporting clients. What happens when orders are late? What if there's an order that can't be fulfilled? How

SHARK BITE

"I always look for vendors that have been through challenging times. I want to work with vendors who are going to be problem solvers, and that means they need to have a history of surviving failures. Those are the vendors who are really going to be able to find solutions."

DAYMOND

do they handle support and technical-related questions? It's important that your vendors are communicative and available, especially in times of hardship. Learn as much as you can about their commitment to service and make sure it aligns with your expectations.

The vendors you choose to work with will have a significant impact on your business, so you'll want to acquire as much information about them as possible. Ask questions; run credit reports; or consult various government agencies, like the Better Business Bureau, about any questionable activities in the vendor's history. The companies you decide to work with will end up playing a crucial role in your business, so be sure to choose wisely.

FINDING YOUR HOME

Before officially launching your company, you must also decide on the physical location your business will call home.

The importance of location and office space will vary depending on the type of organization you're starting. If you're opening a retail store, for example, location is critical, so your options may be more limited. If you're starting a technology company on the other hand, you will have seemingly endless choices. No matter what type of company you're starting, there are many factors to consider.

The first and most common choice is to work from home. This allows you to build your business without the added pressure of extra expenses. For the bootstrapper who's starting a business on the side, working from home may be the very best option. But it isn't without its challenges. When you work from home, you often miss out on the human interactions that occur in a traditional work space. As an entrepreneur you should cultivate your network, and that's not easy to do from a living room.

There are also some financial and logistical hurdles that come with working from home. First, if you plan on writing off your "home office," you need to make sure the space is used *strictly* for work. A rental office space is a full tax write-off, whereas proving the legitimacy of a home office can be a bit more challenging. Additionally, you may need to get supplemental insurance when working from home, because most home owner policies do not cover work-related damages. For example, if your house is broken into and your inventory is stolen, it's unlikely your home owner's insurance will cover it. Make sure you have the necessary protections in place.

If you have a little extra cash to spend and you'd rather not work from your house, you may consider renting an office space. Depending on the resources available in your area, your rental options may range in size and price. Be careful not to get a larger or more luxurious space than you'll actually need. Some business owners make the mistake of thinking they must project a certain image to score bigger deals. While this can occasionally be true in very specific industries, there are plenty of creative ways to get around having to pay double or triple your monthly rent just to impress a potential client. The goal should be to start small and expand as your business does the same.

When renting space, always be particularly mindful of the lease. Starting a new business can be risky and you don't want to get locked into a commitment you can't honor. For instance, you shouldn't sign a two- or three-year lease for a business you've just built. Work with the landlord to come up with terms that make sense for both parties. It's worth paying a little more each month to avoid being stuck in a long and binding contract.

If you live in a major metropolitan city, you may wish to seek out a coworking space. A coworking space is just what it sounds like: a shared work environment. Often made up of entrepreneurs, freelancers, and even a few corporate types, coworking is the new big thing in professional real estate—and there's a good reason why. A great coworking space offers affordable rent, shared resources, and most importantly, a vibrant, well-connected network. Not only can it be a great environment to work from, but it can be the launchpad for your business. Search online and find out if your city has a coworking space that fits your needs. It may just be the perfect solution for your business.

Your final option is to purchase an office space, however most startups are nowhere near ready to make such a commitment in the early stages of building a business. Buying an office is not only a cost-intensive activity; it can also eat up valuable time and energy. Most businesses should wait before attempting to purchase an office space of their own, especially when there are so many other options available.

The location you choose to work from is more than just a building; it's the physical representation of your business. Whether it's a room in your house or an office in a nearby corporate complex, you're going to be spending a lot of time there. Make sure it's somewhere you really enjoy being.

THE BIG BAD LAUNCH

You've evaluated yourself as an entrepreneur, assessed your big idea, and even made it official by incorporating your business. Your vendors are lined up, your office space is chosen, and your product or service is ready to ship. Now it's time to take all that preparation, all that legwork, to the next phase. It's time to transform your effort into action. It's time to launch your business.

First things first: you need to choose a launch date. There are likely to be a number of internal factors that play a role in your public unveiling, and depending on the type of business you're starting, there may be some important external ones too. If you're opening a sweater company, for instance, you probably don't want to launch in the summer. Conversely, if you're starting a swimsuit line, it may be best to avoid the wintertime. Your launch should be as strategic as possible.

Trade shows and events can be great places to launch a new business, as media and potential clients are already gathered together in one place. Many technology companies, for

SHARK BITE

"In this day and age you don't need a fancy, trendy office space to be successful. All you need is a quiet place where you can concentrate and focus. That can be anywhere. It makes sense to do things as inexpensively as possible, so that your time, energy, and money go towards what's really necessary to run the business."

LORI

instance, choose to launch at events like SXSW in Austin, Texas, and Social Media Week in New York City. As a general rule, you'll want to avoid Fridays, as weekends are notorious for killing momentum. You should also stay clear of holidays, even minor ones, as you may need access to a bank or other businesses that could be closed.

Since you've already done plenty of research about your industry and competition, coming up with the sufficient launch date shouldn't be particularly difficult. But no matter which day you choose to share your business with the world, you must first decide if you'll open with a soft launch or a hard launch.

During a soft launch you introduce your business to a select, limited audience. This is good for the kind of business that wants to enter the market slowly. If you're trying to determine whether your business idea is valid (also known as achieving "proof of concept") or you lack the necessary infrastructure required to deliver your product or service on a mass scale, this may be your best option.

One of the great benefits of a soft launch is that it provides additional time to get everything up and running. Whether that involves training staff, building your supply chain, or just getting your financials in order, a soft launch generally provides the company with a bit more breathing room and flexibility. Keep in mind, however, that time works both ways. A soft launch can provide more time to build, but that also means it may take more time to gain customers and start making money.

While many entrepreneurs choose to go with a soft launch, especially if it's their first time starting a business, large corporations that already have resources in place almost always favor a hard launch.

SHARK BITE

"You should always start with a soft launch because it allows you to test your assumptions and see which ones you got right, and more importantly, which ones you got wrong. A big, hard launch is expensive. Getting even one thing wrong can force you to go out of business."

KEVIN

A hard launch is designed to generate as much buzz and as many sales as possible. During a hard launch, all of the marketing efforts are channeled into one coordinated push. Months, if not years, of work go into a hard launch, as everything must be calibrated just right. If you choose to go with a hard launch, it's critical that absolutely everything is in place. The worst thing that can happen during a hard launch is for a small crack in the foundation to sink the entire operation.

Ultimately, it's up to you as the founder to decide which launch strategy is best for your business. If you're ready to make a big splash, a hard launch is your answer. If you want more control, you should probably aim for a soft launch.

Before launching, take a moment to reflect on everything you've achieved thus far. Most people who dream of starting a company never even get to the launch phase. The fact that you've made it this far should be celebrated.

WORK SMART: PRODUCTIVITY HACKS FOR THE MODERN ENTREPRENEUR

Running a small business is not just about working hard; it's about working smart. As your days begin to fill up with tasks, mastering productivity will become more important than it's ever been. While every entrepreneur has his own methods for staying productive, here are three useful hacks that can help you work more efficiently:

Boost willpower by creating better patterns: At one point in time, willpower was thought of as some mysterious, unquantifiable power that one either possessed or didn't. But that theory has since been disproven. As it turns out, willpower is more like a muscle: everyone has it and everyone has the ability to overwork it. So how exactly do you live a productive life without burning out by 3 p.m.? The answer is simple: create better patterns.

When you create patterns, you bypass the decision-making process and avoid tapping into that coveted willpower. Want to get better at working out? Go to the gym every morning for three weeks (the average time it takes to create a habit). Want to get up every morning before your day job to work on your startup? Make it a nonnegotiable commitment for a few weeks. Soon, it will become a daily pattern.

Outsource the time wasters: With so many different services available to help people avoid tasks that waste time and create unhappiness, outsourcing unpleasantries is a great way to become more productive. Whether it's paying bills, sending thank-you cards, or taking your dog for a walk, you can find myriad resources to outsource just about anything you want, some of which are included in the Tools and Resources section in the back of the book.

Although you may not have a lot of extra money to spend on luxuries, there are plenty of ways to outsource on a budget. Make a list of items that weigh you down and do some research on how much it would cost to outsource them. You may be surprised at how affordable it can be to get some of the most time-consuming tasks off your plate.

Prioritize your schedule: Not every task carries the same level of importance. If you want to maximize productivity, you must get in the habit of prioritizing your to-do list and accomplishing things in the appropriate order. It's fine if you want to spend time on that big-picture idea, for instance, but not if there are a hundred little things that need to happen by tomorrow. As each task comes in, assign it a number (one to five)—ones get done first and fives last. As you begin to incorporate this system into your work flow, you'll quickly start to see how it can immediately improve your overall productivity.

10

MASTERING MARKETING

What's the first thing you think of when you hear the word "marketing"? A company brochure? A Twitter page? A radio ad? Maybe you recall that advertising campaign you saw on television or that giveaway promotion on Facebook. If any of these examples popped into your head, you would be correct: they are all forms of marketing. But marketing isn't just a department or campaign; it's a fundamental limb of every business, no matter the size or industry.

According to the American Marketing Association, marketing is defined as "the activity, set of institutions, and processes for creating, communicating, delivering, and exchanging offerings that have value for customers, clients, partners, and society at large." In other words, marketing is the bridge that connects the business to the consumer—the great tightrope of opportunity. And while philosophies may differ on which type of marketing is most effective, every entrepreneur can agree on one thing: marketing matters . . . a lot.

After reading the definition above, you may be wondering what the difference is between marketing, advertising, and public relations (PR). That's a great, and sometimes tricky, question. Talk to a handful of business professionals and you're likely to get a number of different answers. A Fortune 500 CMO, for instance, may describe the breakdown very differently than the owner of a neighborhood mom-and-pop establishment. While the subject could be explored quite extensively, the majority of first-time business owners need only understand one very basic difference.

Marketing generally refers to the overall communication process, as opposed to one specific action. From market research to media strategy, think of marketing as the larger conversation between you and your customer. It is the overarching category, the sum total, of each consumer interaction.

Advertising and PR on the other hand are most often actionable initiatives that help bring a product or service to market, like direct mail or a digital ad buy. That is to say that if marketing is the manufacturing of the ideas, then advertising and PR are the delivery system, which brings the product or service to your audience. While all three are considered to be primary components capable of standing alone, most often advertising and PR are parts of the greater marketing strategy.

SHARK BITE

"The most common mistake that entrepreneurs make when marketing their business is that they try to sell it before going out and getting feedback. If you read the history of any great company, you'll see that most have reinvented their product and audience over and over again, especially in the early stages of the business. You don't know the formula until you get out in real life and test it."

BARBARA

As your company grows and evolves, you may need to develop a more detailed understanding of each element, but for the sake of clarity, in this book the word "marketing" will be used as a blanket term to describe any process or action that connects a business to the outside world.

EMBRACING YOUR BRAND

Another essential element, which often falls under the general marketing category, is branding. A brand is much bigger than just a product or service. It's the emotional response to your business—the visual and psychological representation of your organization's identity.

In more technical terms, branding is "the practice of creating a name, symbol, or design that identifies and differentiates a product from other products." It often combines tangible things like logo, design, and color scheme with more abstract elements like values, goals, and mission. These scattered pieces are woven together to create the overall "vibe" or feel of a business.

When most people think of their favorite product, it's likely they don't actually envision the product itself. Rather, they respond to a feeling the product gives them. Take Coca-Cola, for instance, perhaps the most well-known brand in the world. When you think of Coke, the first thing that comes to mind isn't brown syrup and carbonated water. If that were the case, the beverage company would surely be out of business. No, it's more likely that you imagine the bright red can or the famous ice-skating polar bears. Maybe you even recall a particularly positive memory of something that occurred while you were drinking a Coke. It's not the syrup and water that keeps you coming back for more; it's the brand.

The same can be said for Apple computers. In 2012, *Forbes* magazine valued the Apple brand at $87.1 billion, up 52 percent from two years prior. That's tremendous growth. How did the homegrown technology company become one of the most profitable businesses in the world? Simple. Steve Jobs knew the power of a brand. Like many innovators, Jobs understood that brand needed to be baked into each part of the company and infused in every experience. Moreover, Jobs recognized that a strong brand is the ultimate magnet for loyalty and evangelism because it makes customers feel as though they're participating in more than just a mere exchange of money. Instead, they are connecting to a greater mission. You don't just buy Apple products; you're an "Apple person."

Many small business owners are under the false impression that branding is reserved for larger companies with millions or billions of dollars. But nothing could be further from the truth. In reality, a strong brand requires more creativity than cash—more boldness than budget.

You've already identified your mission; now it's time to go further and infuse it throughout all aspects of your business. What do you believe in as a company? Where did you come from and where are you headed? What truths have you championed as an organization? How do you want people to feel when they think about your company? How do your products or services represent your greater philosophy? As you start to transform these answers into action, your brand, in all its complexity, will slowly begin to emerge.

Remember branding is a dynamic combination of development, design, and experience. It is both your greatest differentiator and ultimate connector. But more importantly, it is the promise you make to each and every customer. And that should never be underrated.

SHARK BITE

"You don't need a large budget to create a strong brand. You need a movement. You need to find the people who are ambassadors for your brand and who will go out and share it with the world. When I started slinging shirts, I found a network of ambassadors who took the brand from city to city. That was what going viral was back then. Today, you can find most of your ambassadors on social networks."

DAYMOND

PREPARING FOR IMPACT

In Chapter Four you learned the value of identifying and cultivating your target market. While knowing this information is helpful when building your business, it's absolutely crucial during the marketing process.

Once you have a clear awareness of your target market, you must next identify which type of marketing is best for *your* business. How can you stand out in a powerful way without wasting time or breaking the bank? While there isn't one surefire strategy, you can increase your chances of accomplishment by pinpointing three key pieces of information.

First you must identify your short- and long-term *marketing goals*. What would your marketing campaign look like if everything went off without a hitch? Details matter, so be sure to get as specific as possible here. Would it bring in a hundred new customers? Would it increase your credibility in the field? Would it open the door to new partnership opportunities? Would it achieve all three? As you'll soon learn, there are many different ways to market your business, and you can't achieve success until you've begun to define it.

Next you must be aware of your *financial limitations*. If

you're starting a new business it's likely your marketing budget will look a lot like your annual salary: nonexistent. Or maybe not. Perhaps you've raised significant capital and have a cool six figures to throw at your marketing needs. While having an abundance of resources is nice, it's not always necessary—and sometimes it can actually get in the way. You don't need a large budget to be a great marketer, but you do need to be exceedingly aware of your restraints.

Finally you must consider your *time frame*. Is the goal to build buzz around a specific launch date or product? Or are you looking to create more long-term awareness? A campaign that produces short-term results will look quite different from one that's designed to stand the test of time. Establishing a time frame will help keep you focused on your efforts and accountable to your goals.

TANK TIP

"Most importantly, you've got to really love what you do. You can't just start a business because you want to work for yourself or somebody else thinks you have a good idea. You've got to love the business with everything you have, even when it ends up taking over your whole life, because eventually it will."

—LANI LAZZARI, FOUNDER OF SIMPLE SUGARS

THE MANY WAYS TO MARKET

Many factors play a role in the success of a marketing campaign. As an entrepreneur, you must not only understand your overall marketing goals, but you must also be able to achieve them in a timely and fiscally responsible manner. From guerrilla and network marketing to direct and affiliate marketing, you can find tens if not hundreds of different marketing strategies. There are, however, a few commonly used channels that every small business owner should comprehend:

Traditional marketing: Offline, or traditional, marketing is still what many people think of when they begin marketing their business. While not always as easy to track and measure, offline marketing is still a productive way to get the word out about your business. Here are a few of the more popular offline methods:

Print: This category includes marketing you may find in any sort of print publication, including newspapers and magazines. Before the days of digital content, print marketing was a popular choice for many businesses. However, in the last few years, entrepreneurs have discovered that they can create their own digital content that is often far more targeted and compelling than any traditional print option. What's more, creating digital content is free or significantly lower in cost. Depending on the size of your budget, print may or may not be a realistic option. But if you do choose to use this technique, be sure to find a publication that resonates with your target market. You never just want to go with the cheapest option.

Television and radio: While television and radio are great ways to gain quick attention, they are often the most cost-prohibitive and least targeted options. With prices that range from thousands to millions of dollars—and that's not even including the cost of production—television and radio are ideal for well-funded small businesses that are looking to execute short-term campaigns geared toward building quick buzz. You may consider this type of medium if you're holding a large event, for instance, or running some sort of substantial promotion.

Direct mail: Although occasionally thought of as old-fashioned, direct mail can still be a productive tool for certain types of businesses. Direct mail is nothing more than unsolicited advertising sent through the mail. Usually involving items such as flyers, brochures, and postcards, a direct mail campaign often centers around one particular call to action (e.g., "Call now for 3 months of free service"). While in theory this marketing strategy can provide you with one-on-one access to your target audience, you may find it difficult to stay out of the junk mail pile. Price out a direct mail campaign and then decide if it's worth the effort. You may have more luck with email marketing, which you'll read about below.

Digital marketing: Thanks to its low price point and high engagement, many small business owners consider digital marketing to be the most effective and attractive option. Once dominated by banner ads and affiliate programs, today digital marketing features an ever-increasing number of options for the small business owner. You may wish to combine a few of these campaigns in your larger marketing plan:

Social media: By now the term "social media" has become a standard part of the everyday vernacular, but it wasn't so long ago that this popular communication tool was still relatively unknown. From Facebook and Twitter to Pinterest and LinkedIn, social media has become one of the most important ways to market a product or service. With more than 340 million tweets sent each day, and Facebook accounting for one out of every seven minutes spent online, finding a captive audience for your business isn't hard. Social media's greatest strength, however, is also its greatest weakness. With so many companies vying for attention, it's easy to get lost in the shuffle. When developing your social media strategy, be sure to find compelling ways to differentiate yourself from the crowd. If you want people to care about your business, you must give them a reason to.

Email marketing: Think of email marketing as the digital equivalent of direct mail: the use of email to promote and market a product. While this can be a great way to get attention, it relies heavily on your ability to build a database of targeted consumers. If your company sells sirloin steaks, for instance, you won't have much use for a list of one thousand vegetarians. While you can purchase mailing lists from various companies, it's better to develop your own list via your website and social channels. It's always more productive to engage in a conversation with people who actually want to hear from you.

Search engine marketing: Both powerful and effective in its own way, search engine marketing (SEM) is the process of gaining traffic on or visibility from search engine results pages. This type of marketing is typically split into two distinct areas: search engine optimization (SEO) and pay-per-click (PPC). Don't let all the technical jargon confuse you; if executed well, SEM can provide huge results.

According to industry experts, search engine optimization (SEO) is a "methodology of strategies, techniques, and tactics used to increase the amount of visitors to a website by obtaining a high-ranking placement in the search results page of a search engine." In other words, it's a way to increase your visibility on search sites like Google, Bing, and Yahoo! by making specific changes to your website. Outside the potential cost of hiring an SEO expert, this is a free way to acquire more traffic.

Pay-per-click (PPC) is also a form of online marketing designed to direct traffic to a website, but using this model, businesses purchase ads on search engines and pay a certain amount each time the ad is clicked. To see PPC in action, go to Google and type in any search term related to your business. If you're selling purple hats, for instance, search for "purple hats." Do you see all the ads on the sidebar to the right? That's paid search engine marketing in action. The price for this type of marketing ranges, depending on the popularity of the keywords you wish to be associated with.

Content marketing: A general term for all marketing formats that involve developing, creating, and distributing content with the goal of engaging consumers, content marketing is one of the most effective ways to build long-term consumer engagement. Defined by the Content Marketing Institute as "the art of communicating with your customers and prospects without selling," content marketing is popular among organizations of all shapes and sizes with a variety of budgets and objectives. While most people think of this type of marketing as involving strictly written content, it also includes video, audio, and other types of media that engage consumers. For instance, a company blog, YouTube channel, or podcast are all examples of content marketing.

Whether you choose to market your business online or offline, you'll want to be sure to create milestones along the way to test whether or not your efforts are in fact successful. In a digital marketing campaign those milestones may be directly related to response or click-through rates. For instance, if you advertise on a search engine like Google and your ad gets five clicks for every one hundred times it's displayed, that would mean you have a 5 percent click-through rate. But is 5 percent a good number? Maybe. There are numerous factors that play a role in evaluating a click-through rate, many of which are specific to your type of business.

More important than click-through, however, is actual engagement. For example, how much are your fans/followers interacting with your social media platforms? Who's reading your emails? How many people are signing up for your mail-

SHARK BITE

"How you market your business depends on what kind of product or service you're selling. You have to go where your target customers are. Personally, I like to cast as wide of a net as possible and hit as many channels as I can. The more people who know about you, the more your service or product will be talked about and shared."

LORI

ing list or opting in to offers? It's critical that you understand your industry's standards for success and closely measure both your digital and traditional marketing campaigns to make sure you meet them.

While it's likely you'll end up focusing your efforts on a few different channels, many marketing experts believe that taking a holistic approach to the process is the best way to achieve success. That being said, most small businesses don't have the budget or time to aggressively market their product or service in such a comprehensive way, at least not at first. So it's important to focus on creating a plan that works for your business.

POWERHOUSE PUBLIC RELATIONS

The goal of any marketing plan is to gain the attention of new customers and spotlight the business in a compelling, thoughtful, and relevant way. While advertising and promotions can certainly accomplish that, relying solely on these methods can be both cost-prohibitive and inefficient. That's why every small business should also develop some sort of public relations (PR) strategy.

According to the Public Relations Society of America (PRSA),

Media Kit Checklist

There are no distinct rules to follow when creating a great media kit, except that it should be a good representation of your brand and include the following:

☐ Company history
☐ Compelling facts about the business
☐ Available products and services
☐ Founder's bio
☐ High-resolution photos (a couple)

You may also wish to include the following:
☐ Testimonials
☐ Business-related statistics
☐ Screenshots of your digital assets (website, social media, etc.).

Be wary, however, of making your media kit too long or extensive. The goal is to educate, not overwhelm.

public relations is "a strategic communication process that builds mutually beneficial relationships between organizations and their publics." Not only can PR often reach more people than traditional advertising, it can lead to a more credible type of awareness, making it a potent weapon for any company.

Even if you don't have the time or money to develop a full-blown PR strategy, it's still possible to actively promote your business by committing to a few simple actions.

First, before looking for a media opportunity, you'll want to create a media kit. A media kit is a packet of information that tells the story of your business in a concise and visually appealing way. While its main purpose is to provide the press with information about your company, it can also be used to educate customers and partners.

Don't make the mistake of waiting to create a media kit until one is requested of you. Your media kit is an embodiment of both you and your company. If it's thrown together at the last minute, it will most likely lack the necessary polish and professionalism.

Next, you may wish to consider issuing a press release. Designed to alert the media of something new or noteworthy, a press release is a good way to earn coveted media coverage. But press releases only work if your outreach is specific. For instance, you wouldn't want to send a press release about your recent commitment to sustainable energy to every single media contact in your database. Instead, you would get much better results by sending it to a handful of influential environmental contacts who might be able to actually do something with the news. Otherwise, you'll just be inundating reporters with irrelevant stories that don't apply to their particular outlet, which just wastes everyone's time—including your own.

When writing a press release, be honest, clever, and to the point; this isn't a place for hyperbole. People in the media get more press releases than they know what to do with, which makes them naturally skilled at seeing through distortion and exaggeration.

One of the best ways to get people interested in your business is to get them interested in *you*. Therefore it's always a good idea to find unique ways to position yourself as an expert in your particular industry. You may sometimes hear this concept go by another name: thought leadership.

Thanks to the rise of digital communication, becoming a thought leader is now more achievable than ever before. While there are numerous routes to explore, some methods are more accessible than others. Developing original content, for instance, is perhaps the best way to begin the process.

Whether it's through guest blogging, producing podcasts, or writing e-books, there are myriad ways to create highly engaging, relevant content. Although content creation can require significant time, it's almost always worth the investment.

Another popular way of becoming a thought leader is to ramp up your public speaking. From conferences to events, there are a number of speaking opportunities that can help increase your visibility and notoriety. Becoming an expert can help your business achieve significant growth, so it's worth devoting some solid effort to the task.

Finally, depending on your type of business, you may discover that creating experiences around your product or service is an effective way to gain media attention. In other words, if you want a story, try doing something story-worthy. Let's say, for example, that you own a tutoring company that caters to high school students. Instead of trying to create a pitch around your new educational product, you may garner more attention by hosting an event that brings together a panel of esteemed college admission experts for an evening of conversation. Events and experiences are a great way to attract more attention, but always make sure they align with your business goals and speak to your target market.

A well-planned and thoughtfully executed PR strategy can boost your business and save you precious time and resources. It can also position your business in a way that establishes trust and credibility, which helps to attract new customers and build loyalty with your current base.

Of course, having something to say is only the first part of gaining media attention. The next and most important part is getting someone, the right someone, to listen. With so many companies hungry for the spotlight, learning to pitch the media is crucial to your success. Similar to what you learned about pitching to investors, it requires confidence, knowledge, and good, old-fashioned fortitude. However, pitching to the media also sometimes demands an extra layer of creativity and panache. Here are a few ways to improve your chances of getting recognized:

Avoid long emails: Just as your media kit should be brief and to the point, so too should any pitch you make. Think about it from the recipient's perspective. Writers and editors are constantly inundated with pitches; they don't have time to read four paragraphs of content before learning what it is you're trying to sell. A couple compelling paragraphs about why you're reaching out and what your company does is all you need to pique interest.

Make the subject line catchy: While you should never be dishonest when pitching, it's important that your email has a catchy and compelling subject line. Again, because an editorial team receives so many pitches, it's likely your email may never even be opened. You'll increase your chances of getting noticed by coming up with clever ways to stand out in the inbox.

Try not to be obnoxious: The best way *not* to get your story picked up is to come across as needy, annoying, or high-maintenance. While most writers appreciate tenacity, there is a clear line between diligent and annoying. It's fine to follow up once, but after that assume it's not going to happen and back off. Getting a reputation for being obnoxious will follow you longer than you think.

Stay relevant: You probably wouldn't want to pitch a beauty editor about a motorcycle product. Likewise, you wouldn't want to pitch an automotive magazine about a beauty product. Thinking outside of the box is encouraged, but only if it's within reason. Similar to how your business should be built around solving a consumer's problem, your pitch should be

SHARK BITE

"It's really easy to get the email and social media handles of people in the media who have influence. Find them, and give those people a reason to talk about you."

MARK

designed to solve the writer or editor's problem. They have deadlines. They need content. You have a story to tell. You're already halfway there. Keep your pitches relevant and focused, and help them solve their biggest problem: finding compelling stories to share with their readers.

Don't pitch cold: Relationships are a fundamental part of every business. The most effective way to get a story published is to already have established a connection with the writer or editor *before* you need press. Start building relationships today so you can avoid the cold call tomorrow.

FROM SHARING TO SELLING:
SOCIAL NETWORKS AS A MARKETING TOOL

With 56 percent of Americans on at least one social network, it's likely you have a personal profile on Facebook, Twitter, or one of the many other social platforms that pop up every day. But does your business have the same sort of online social presence?

Social media is hands down one of the most vibrant and effective marketing tools available to an entrepreneur. It's free, powerful, and full of rich, comprehensive data about your target market—the perfect storm for marketing success.

But perhaps more important than how social media helps you is how it helps your audience *find* you. Consider this: 91 percent of local searchers say they use Facebook to find local businesses online and 71 percent of social media users say they are more likely to purchase from a brand they are connected with. What exactly does this mean for you? Simply put, consumers are beginning to *expect* that the businesses they support will have a social presence. And you know what they say: the customer is always right.

But there's more to social media success than just setting up a profile page. Like any tool, it can only be effective when you learn how to use it. The biggest mistake businesses make when joining a social network is that they view it merely as an advertising tool. Yes, social media does offer many interesting advertising opportunities, but at its core that's not really what it's about. It may sound hokey, but social media is about connection and engagement; it's about building solid relationships and leveraging those relationships to achieve your business goals. And the only way to do that is to engage in real, authentic conversations.

Engaging in authentic conversations means you don't just talk; you must also be willing to listen, really listen, to what your audience is saying. Think of it like having a conversation in real life. If you walk up to someone and just start yapping, it's likely that sooner or later the person will walk away. The same is true on any social network. You must learn how to talk and listen, initiate and respond.

The next most common pitfall that many businesses stumble into is that they lack focus. You don't need to be on Facebook, Twitter, Pinterest, Instagram, Google Plus, Vine, LinkedIn, and every other social network in the world to be successful. It's much more effective to concentrate your efforts on two or three of the mediums that suit your company best.

If your audience consists mainly of consumers (as opposed to businesses), for instance, Facebook is probably where you want to spend most of your time. With 23 percent of users checking their account at least five times a day, and 47 percent of social network users saying Facebook has the greatest impact on their purchases, Facebook can have a major affect on your business. But it isn't your only option.

Another great choice for businesses selling directly to consumers is Twitter. Often preferred by organizations that want a more casual, fast-paced conversation with their audience, this 140-character platform provides companies with a quick, real-time way to connect with their audience on a regular basis.

For businesses whose audience is primarily made up of other businesses, the best option may be LinkedIn. With over 100 million users, it's estimated that LinkedIn is 277 percent more effective at generating business leads than other social networks. With features like LinkedIn Groups, LinkedIn Answers, and Targeted Product Tags, this is a great solution for business owners looking to connect with other businesses.

Whichever social network you choose to invest in, remember that what you're making is in fact an investment. Like any marketing effort, it's all about what you put into the process, so you shouldn't expect to see results right away. Choose the platform that makes the most sense for your business and put a little time into it each day. Before you know it you'll have your own robust community.

11

LEARNING TO SELL

Earl Tupper had a problem: his product wasn't selling. Although he knew he'd created something of tremendous value, he couldn't figure out how to get people to actually open their wallets. And that was particularly troubling to Tupper because he'd always prided himself on his ability to sell just about anything. In fact, prior to becoming an inventor, Tupper was a career salesman, starting when he was just ten years old. But this time he was at a loss. Because his product was so innovative, he would first have to convince the world they needed it—and that was no easy feat. Two years after he started the company, things were still looking bleak.

But then something happened. One day, quite out of the blue, Tupper started to notice that sales were beginning to pick up. He couldn't figure out why. He hadn't altered his strategy or received any new press. In fact, not much had changed at all. Why was inventory all of the sudden moving?

He began to look at the data behind the numbers and noticed something strange: the sales weren't coming from everyday consumers but from a direct-sales company that had developed their own unique approach. They were recruiting local reps to throw parties at their homes and demonstrate the product to friends and family. In fact, the sales strategy worked so well that Tupper eventually decided to adopt it himself. Not long after, Earl Tupper sold his company and made millions. Today, over fifty years later, Tupperware is still a household name.

Earl Tupper's story highlights an important lesson: you can have the greatest, most groundbreaking product in the world, but if you can't sell it, your business will ultimately fail. In other words, to be an entrepreneur you must first be a salesperson.

Selling gets a bad rap. When most people think of the typical "salesperson," they see a fast-talking, oily-haired hustler trying to swindle a nice old lady out of her hard-earned money. They picture the old-fashioned door-to-door type, complete with fake grin and cheap suit, who interrupts dinner with exaggerated tales and false promises. They see the knife set that's been collecting dust, the used car they shouldn't have bought, and the pyramid scheme they almost fell for. Most people view the act of selling as a negative—a manipulative and one-sided transaction. But that's not selling at all, at least it's not good selling.

Selling is nothing more than providing someone with a product or service that will enhance or improve her life. And whether your job description includes the word "sales" or not, you are in fact in the business of selling. Each day you must sell a hundred different things: an idea to a coworker, a restaurant recommendation to a spouse, a goal or resolution to yourself. You may not realize it, but the average person spends the majority of his day trying to sell one thing or another. So it only makes sense to learn how to sell in smarter, more effective ways.

SHARK BITE

"It all comes down to what you can do for the customer. Great salespeople are not pushy, but they're not wallflowers either. You have to understand what makes the customer tick, which means listening. It's not about what you say; it's about how you make people feel. Buying and selling are not rational decisions; they're emotional decisions. And anytime you can appeal to someone on an emotional level and make a connection, you're halfway there."

ROBERT

BREAKING DOWN THE BARRIERS

The first step to becoming a better salesperson is getting past those pesky mental barriers that stand in the way—the most prominent of which is the fear of failure. Luckily, there's an easy way to overcome this one: just accept it. Accept that you will fail. A lot. Guaranteed. And since you can do absolutely nothing to prevent it, you might as well learn to accept it from the start.

The Beatles were turned away by almost every label in the United Kingdom. Steven Spielberg was rejected by film schools three times. Walt Disney was fired from his first newspaper job for lacking imagination. Failure is nothing more than a prelude to success—and a poetic one at that. It puts your work in perspective, strengthens your will, and makes you an all-around better entrepreneur. Simply put, the quicker you learn to fail, the faster you'll begin to achieve. As Lori Greiner says, "Success is not final. Failure is not fatal. It is the courage to continue that counts."

Another common barrier is a lack of preparation. As you'll learn in this section, selling is a process that requires considerable groundwork. You should never walk into a room cold—especially in an age where information is so freely available.

Even if you're naturally charismatic or a good communicator, even if you're generally fearless and daring, a great salesperson must be wise enough to recognize the value of preparation and readiness.

The final barrier is often the most difficult to define and hardest to fix, as it's directly related to one's self-worth. To sell anything you must first and foremost believe you are capable of doing it. Although that may sound like a simple enough task, you'd be surprised at the mental fortitude it can require.

One of the biggest struggles first-time business owners face is a lack of self-assurance. It's natural of course to feel uncertain about something you've never done before. But the only way to convince others you're worth investing in is to invest in yourself first. That means never undercutting your value, discounting your abilities, or feeling guilty for demanding your worth. It means walking into a room not as a hobbyist or amateur, but as a professional who is just as worthy of being there as anyone else.

Recognize that you will make mistakes; understand that selling requires tremendous time and care; accept that you are worthy of achievement. Only once you've done each of those will you ever be able to embrace your role as a salesperson and begin closing deals.

SHARK BITE

"Being a good salesperson is about having a natural passion and love for what you're selling. You've got to have that. People can sense that passion, and that will get them excited about your product. You have to genuinely believe in what you're selling. The consumer is very savvy."

LORI

THE EVOLVING SALES PROCESS

Assuming your business is centered on a product (as opposed to a service), you'll either be selling to a consumer, retailer, or distributor. You may even be selling to all three. And while the ultimate goal is the same, to close a deal, the process behind each varies greatly.

Consumer: When selling directly to a consumer you essentially have three channels to consider: online, via your own brick-and-mortar store, or through some type of event, like a tradeshow or market. The obvious benefits of selling your product directly is that you retain complete control of the experience and improve your margins. Not having to share the profits with an outside retailer or distributor can do wonders for your bottom line. But, of course, this strategy also presents many challenges—the most common of which is gaining awareness. For consumers to patronize your business they must first know you exist. That means your brand must be strong and compelling enough to stand on its own. Otherwise, you could have difficulty attracting new customers, which is why many companies choose to sell through retailers or distributors. **EXAMPLE:** Cousins Maine Lobster's business is segmented across three thriving direct-to-consumer channels: e-commerce, food truck, and pop-up restaurant. Selling this way allows the lobster company to offer a competitive price while also maintaining a healthy profit margin.

Retail: Selling to individual retailers can certainly be an effective way to get your product to market, but it can also take considerable time and effort. Depending on whether you're selling to a franchise or independent business, you could find yourself bombarded with requests for meetings and pitches—many of which won't necessarily lead to a high volume of sales. What's more, many retailers, especially franchise operations, prefer to go through distributors as it's often the quickest and least painful way to purchase inventory. It's easier to make one, larger transaction than five smaller ones. Therefore, the best option for many businesses is to work with a distributor. **EXAMPLE:** One of Lani Lazzari's main goals for Simple Sugars is to gain national distribution in a major retail chain like Sephora. This would not only increase sales but also help build the brand.

Distributors: A distributor has relationships with a network of retailers, which means your product has the potential to reach a larger audience. However, it also means that both the distributor and retailer are making money off your product, which of course affects your profits. Still, working with a distributor may be a wise option; a smaller percentage of something is better than a larger percentage of nothing. In order to attract a distributor, it's important to have a scalable product that doesn't cost too much to fulfill. The goal for a distributor is mass. They may also be more attracted to a business with a line of products, as opposed to one single product. **EXAMPLE:** On the ReadeREST website, distributors can purchase a high volume of inventory at a lower price point. While the eyewear company may not make as much money per unit, working with a distributor on a larger order will bring a concentrated flow of cash into the business and help achieve scale.

While selling directly to the consumer is generally less expensive and easier to execute, there isn't one clear path to success. As technology continues to evolve, so too does the sales process, creating more opportunities for businesses of all size. Still, even though the Internet is changing the game, there's value in understanding the traditional sales cycle, which can be broken down into seven major parts:

Prospecting: If you wish to gain customers, you must know where to find them. In other words, your first step should be to identify and cultivate potential leads. Let's say, for instance, that you've started a landscaping business and you're targeting local business owners who own more than one property. While you may not have a surplus of those folks in your immediate network, it's likely you regularly interact with people who do. Discovering qualified prospects is a never-ending process and should be a major priority for every business owner.

Planning: Oprah believes that luck is what happens when opportunity meets preparation. And you know what? She's absolutely right. While you don't often have control over the opportunity part, preparation is 100 percent your responsibility—and one you must take with the utmost seriousness. Before approaching a customer, make sure you're as prepared as possible. Spend significant time researching the needs and challenges of your potential consumer, and be sure to include those points in your pitch. The greatest way to determine future behaviors is through the examination of past behaviors, so try to know as much as possible about your lead's history.

Approach: Think of this step like a first date. The immediate goal isn't to propose marriage; it's to begin building a relationship. When you make an initial approach, be sure not to come on too strong. You don't need to seal the deal right away. You need to first build rapport, establish a friendly connection, and begin the conversation. Try to put yourself in the customer's shoes. When you visit a retail store, for example, how do you feel when an associate immediately rushes over and begins pitching you on the latest sale? It's too much, too soon, right? Instead, it's far more effective when you're greeted with a casual approach and eased into the purchasing process.

Needs assessment: Since the entrepreneur and the salesperson are actually the same individual, their ultimate goal should be the same: to solve a problem. After you've established an initial connection, the next step is to assess specific needs that the particular customer may have. This is probably the most important part of the sales process, as it provides critical insight into how your product or service fits in the customer's life. During this step, you'll want to ask smart, broad questions that allow you to gain as much insight as possible. For example, it would be wise to identify the customers' business goals and uncover any challenges their organization faces. This way, you'll be able to tailor your pitch directly to their specific needs.

Presentation: Now that you've established a connection and assessed any specific needs, it's time to pitch. Don't waste your energy trying to sell the features. Instead focus on how your product or service can solve the customer's specific problem(s). Going back to the landscaping business, the customer doesn't care if you have high-powered, top-of-the-line equipment. That's only interesting to you. However, superior equipment probably means you can perform the job faster and more efficiently than the competitor, which will ultimately save the customer money. Now, *that's* interesting. Always frame the pitch around the consumer's needs, not your own.

The close: Of all the steps in the sales process, this is the one that's most often botched. Although there are many famous closing "techniques," closing a deal isn't about trickery or manipulation. If you've masterfully executed the previous steps and established a baseline of trust, the close should be seamless. When you have your customers' best interest at heart, a good close goes back to the original goal of solving a problem. Perhaps they're concerned about the financial investment or the timing. Maybe they have doubts about the product or service itself. During the closing process, it's your job to honestly and accurately acknowledge any lingering concerns and work with your customers—not against them—to solve those problems. The days of closing at all costs are over. If you've effectively discovered the customer's needs and laid out a viable solution, acquiring a commitment shouldn't be difficult.

Follow-up: Closing a deal isn't the end of a relationship; it's the beginning. Maintaining communication is crucial to the long-term success of any customer relationship. Once a sale is closed, it's your job to make sure the customer has a pleasant experience and that all expectations are met with precision and care. Find creative ways to regularly follow up with customers and show that you're genuinely interested in their satisfaction. Relationships are the heart of any business, and you want to make sure yours are strong and prosperous.

SHARK BITE

"To be a good salesperson you must be willing to tell the truth and put yourself in the shoes of the customer. You have to understand why the customer would want to buy from you, and then help them understand why they should."

MARK

THE ART OF NEGOTIATION

While the sales process is rarely linear, there are certain parts that will always remain constant, like the close. And no matter if you're a veteran salesperson or new to the game, your ability to secure a lucrative deal comes down to how well you can negotiate.

The art of negotiation is a fine one, with many subtle intricacies. There are, however, a few helpful tips and tricks that anyone can use to instantly become a better negotiator.

As with many parts of running a business, the first step is always preparation. Before the negotiation process begins, it's important to have as much information about the deal as possible. What exactly are you trying to sell? What is your absolute minimum selling price? Who is the decision maker who must be in the room for the deal to close? Once you have an answer to these questions, you'll be able to frame the conversation in a more productive way.

Next, you must have a comprehensive understanding of the value you're providing. Particularly in service businesses, people try to sell the value of their time, as opposed to the value of their impact. But if you're helping a company bring in an extra $5 million, it doesn't matter if it takes you ten days or ten weeks, you're adding significant value to the operation and you have the right to capitalize on that.

You must also learn to listen carefully and respond only to the questions being asked. You've seen this happen all the time on *Shark Tank*: an entrepreneur is asked a question, and instead of really listening to what's being said, he goes on a tangent and reveals something unsavory about the business or himself. Negotiation is a delicate process and requires laser focus. Above all else, stay concentrated on the goal.

Finally, whether you're negotiating with a large corporation or a single individual, you must be willing to walk away. Even if you need the money, even if you're hungry for the business, if a deal isn't in your best interest you must not be afraid to turn it down. Being motivated to close a deal is great, but not if it ends up ultimately hurting your business.

TANK TIP

"Google should be your best friend. If you learn to search properly and are willing to spend the time exploring, I believe it can teach you more than any business school ever could. Call it Google equity."

—MOSHE WEISS, FOUNDER OF SOUNDBENDER

NETWORKING LIKE A PRO

Knowing how and when to initiate the right conversation is paramount, but you must also know with *whom* to initiate the conversation. Improving your networking skills is one of the best ways to become a better salesperson.

Similar to how some view sales, when most people think of "networking" they imagine some poorly lit conference room full of slick and sleazy businessmen hurriedly pacing about, shaking hands and exchanging cards with any poor soul who happens upon their path. But don't let that outdated approach to networking turn you off from the activity.

Networking is about adding value. Period. It has nothing to do with how *they* can help *you*. Quite the opposite. It's about how *you* can help *them*. How can you make someone else's project that much better? How can you find a solution to a challenge that person has been stuck on?

The primary goal of networking is to position yourself as an important and respected resource. Approaching networking this way not only makes the process more advantageous for both parties; it also builds goodwill and credibility, which isn't an easy thing to do.

This idea may seem backwards if you're used to viewing networking merely as an opportunity to self-promote. But if your goal is to build long-term, meaningful relationships, approaching networking from a place of generosity and authenticity is really your only choice.

Below you'll find a handful of tips and tricks designed to help you improve your networking abilities. Try to apply some of these the next time you find yourself at an event.

Do some digging: In the digital age there's no excuse for being underprepared. Do preliminary research on some of the people who will be in attendance. Using a combination of social media and offline resources, there are usually plenty of ways to uncover who you may encounter. You won't be able to have productive conversations with everyone, so choose three or four people to target and focus your research around them. Remember: it's about the quality of the relationship, not the quantity. Find out where a person went to school, her work history, maybe even something about her personal life. You never want to come off as creepy, but being informed about a person's work and life will make it that much easier to make the most of your time with her.

Talk less; listen more: The next time you go to a conference, spend five minutes in the hotel bar, and you're guaranteed to hear it: the gentle hums and murmurs of countless me, me, me's and I, I, I's. For whatever reason, most people think that good networking is about talking. But the best networkers know it's really all about listening. In fact, the right ratio should be somewhere around 80/20—20 percent talking, 80 percent listening. When you listen, really listen, to what the other person is saying, you're able to quickly deduce how you can best add value to the relationship. What's more, you're giving someone the opportunity to do what most people love best: talk about themselves. By asking smart questions and showing legitimate interest, you're likely to come across as likeable and smart.

Follow up: When it comes to networking, this is the place where most people fumble. After establishing a new connection, you should immediately follow up. In fact, you should do so within the first twelve to twenty-four hours. Depending on the specifics of your interaction, most often a simple email will suffice. In it, you should remind the contact where you met, touch on what you spoke about, and fulfill any promises you may have made. Again, you're trying to establish yourself as a resource—nothing more. Here's an example of what a typical follow-up note might look like:

Hi Bob,

It was great meeting you tonight at the Shark Tank Jump Start Your Business *book launch event. I was excited to hear about all that you've achieved with your new business. It sounds like you're really on the right track.*

As promised, I'll make sure to connect you tomorrow morning with my contact over at XYZ Beverage Company. I think he may be a really great person for you to know.

Good luck with everything, and please do stay in touch. Looking forward to connecting again soon.

Best,
Michael Parrish DuDell

SHARK BITE

"The most important part of building a strong network is finding like-minded people who share the same mission. It's people and information that are the most priceless commodities, not product."

DAYMOND

Keep detailed records: Not only does a great networker spend more time listening than she does talking, she also knows the value of recording her insights and keeping detailed records. It's important to keep track of whom you meet, when you meet them, and what you speak about. You may also wish to include any observations you make during the encounter. For instance, if you overhear your new contact tell the waiter she doesn't drink, that would be something worth noting. This way, should you ever meet outside the office, you know to suggest coffee, not wine. It may sound small, but it's often the little things that can make a big difference.

LOOKING AHEAD: FORECASTING SALES

You hear it all the time on *Shark Tank*: "What kind of sales are you projecting next quarter? How much do you think you can sell next year?" Those numbers don't just come out of thin air; they are the result of careful consideration and analysis.

Forecasting sales is the process of estimating your growth by carefully examining three key areas: consumer demand, market conditions, and previous performance. Although many unknown factors can influence your projections, the goal is always to come up with the most accurate estimations possible.

There are many ways to forecast sales, and larger companies have entire teams dedicated to the task. As a small business owner, however, it's unlikely you'll have the access to or the need for these kinds of heavy-hitting resources. But that doesn't mean you're excused from the task altogether. Forecasting is crucial to staying on track and meeting your sales targets. Below you'll find four easy steps to help you get started:

Step One: Project your run-rate: Although it may have a fancy name, a run-rate projection simply predicts how much your company will earn over a period of time. Most often this is done by using quarterly numbers to project annual revenue. For instance, if you made $25,000 in your first quarter, your run-rate projection for the year would be $100,000. While you can use this data to forecast far into the future, the farther you go, the less accurate the numbers will be.

Step Two: Examine past trends and future indicators: Next, you must dig deeper and examine any changes that have occurred that could affect future business. Has your product or service evolved? Have you added or subtracted features? And if so, how have your customers responded to these changes? Speaking of customers, how fast is your base growing? How much is it costing you to acquire each customer? What factors can expedite or impede future growth? When performing this assessment, pay special attention to three factors: customers, products, and price.

Step Three: Evaluate the current market: Before you can control the market, you must first understand it. What are the latest trends affecting your product? How has your consumer evolved since you first launched? Has the market grown or shrunk? At this point, you must also look outside your company to the competition. Is your competition increasing or decreasing? What innovations are your competitors investing in that could lead to greater market share? What opportunities are they missing? Performing a thorough evaluation of the market will give you a better sense of where your industry is headed and how your business should grow.

Step Four: Factor in future plans: In this final step, you'll want to include any strategic business plans you may have for the future. Are you being featured in a large publication next quarter? Are you planning to launch a new product or service within the year? Are you doing a big seasonal promotion or changing your pricing strategy? This data will play a substantial role in your growth and revenue earnings.

By following these four steps, you'll be able to make a more accurate projection of future sales. While technically you can perform forecasts many years in advance, that's probably not necessary for your business. As industries change and grow, so too do sales cycles. That is to say that innovation is fluid, not static. And since innovation is crucial to the development of your business, you'll probably only need to perform sales forecasting up to two years in advance, unless of course you find the task to be particularly enjoyable.

RICK HOPPER, READEREST (SEASON 3)

BIG IDEA: A simple solution for losing track of eyewear that keeps glasses within hands reach, safely and securely

INVESTOR: Lori Greiner

There are some people who are born to be entrepreneurs—people who, from their very first memories, have been hungrily searching for solutions to problems big and small. Rick Hopper is one of those people.

"I had vision as a little kid," says Rick. "As soon as I learned mathematics, I understood the power of information, and since then I've always wanted more."

Rick was the middle child in the family, so on outings he always found himself squished between his two brothers in the backseat of his parents' 1973 Ford Pinto.

"If you've ever sat in the back of a 1973 Ford Pinto station wagon, you know there's a really uncomfortable bump right in the middle," Rick recounts. "That was my seat!"

As a result, Rick would spend most of the car rides perched forward, staring at the gauges on the dashboard.

"My eyes would dart between the speedometer, odometer,

and clock," says Rick. "I was constantly trying to figure out exactly how long it would take to get to a destination. I always had numbers running in my head."

Although Rick wouldn't start his first company until much later, he never wasted an opportunity to exercise his entrepreneurial muscle. No matter his salary or position, he was always searching for ways to improve systems, solve problems, and create a stronger business. "Looking back," recalls Rick, "I think I probably drove my bosses crazy."

Eventually Rick opened his first business and ran it successfully for ten years before deciding to sell the company. Not long after, Rick's doctor broke the news that he would need to start wearing glasses. Rick didn't know it yet, but the seed for his next business had just been planted.

Very quickly, Rick discovered that wearing glasses was a pain. When he took them off, he never had a good place to put them. And if he tucked them into his shirt, they always wound up falling on the floor and getting scratched.

After a long conversation about this problem with his best friend, Rick decided it was up to him to create a solution: a magnetized system that allowed a person to hang a pair of glasses safely and conveniently on any shirt. His goal wasn't to create a business; he was simply trying to solve his own problem. But very soon it became clear that the problem was bigger than just him.

"Every single day I got stopped on the street by people who wanted to know how my glasses were staying on my shirt," says Rick. "It was very clear that the demand was there."

After many of his customers suggested he go on *Shark Tank*, Rick finally decided to take the plunge, and eventually he secured a deal with Lori Greiner. The rest, as they say, is history.

"Thank God I had some experience with a rapidly growing company, or I never would have been able to handle what happened after *Shark Tank*," says Rick. "It was like being on a helicopter and getting dropped into a monster wave. You either sink or swim."

Rick chose to swim, and has loved every minute of it.

"I have a theory that if you're lucky enough to get more in life, you always get more of the same. If you're miserable, all that extra responsibility, opportunity, and chaos will lead to more misery. If you're happy, you'll find even more happiness. I've always been a really happy guy—right down to my core. And *Shark Tank* has given me more of the same. I couldn't imagine anything better."

To find out more about ReadeREST, visit ReadeREST.com or follow them on Twitter @readerest.

REAL-WORLD WISDOM: "No matter how excited you are about an idea, you've got to do the math and count the costs. There are so many little things that need to happen to get a product to market, and those little things can add up. You owe it to yourself to count the costs before starting a business."

PART FIVE
TAKING IT TO THE
NEXT LEVEL

BARBARA CORCORAN

CLAIM TO FAME: Real estate mogul who turned a $1,000 loan into a multi-million dollar real estate empire.

THE WAY I WORK: "For me it always comes down to the entrepreneur. All I need is the right person, and I can make a business successful."

THE POWER OF FAILURE

'm great at failing—there's no doubt about it. It's my sweet spot. In fact, my best ideas usually come from some type of failure. And I think that's true of every entrepreneur—at least it's true of the ones I've invested in on *Shark Tank* who have done well. And it's lacking in every entrepreneur I've invested in that isn't succeeding. That's the dividing line.

We all fail, but the people who ultimately succeed are the ones who take no time to feel sorry for themselves. The truth is that when most people take a major hit, they quietly go out of business. They may look like they're still in business—they're at their desk every day—but mentally they're out of business, because they're spending all their time licking their wounds. You can't lick your wounds if you want to be an entrepreneur. You have to be able to continuously jump back up and say, "Hit me again! Hit me again!"

Everyone talks about tenacity and perseverance, and those are important, but I think the element that's really critical is having the *inability* to feel sorry for yourself. Because so many people do.

When an entrepreneur walks into the tank, it's not the

company I'm looking at; it's the person. That's it. I'll even take a bad idea intentionally and turn it around because I know I have the right entrepreneur. I'll take the bad idea with the right entrepreneur any day of the week. And, of course, to be a good entrepreneur you need the talent, enthusiasm, and energy, but you also must have the ability to deal with failure.

12

YOU CAN'T DO IT ALONE: BUILDING THE RIGHT TEAM

While many business owners are mavericks at heart, most reach a point where they need to start thinking about building a team. Whether you have a retail operation or a small tech startup, hiring employees comes with both benefits and challenges. Adding the right employees at the right time can take an organization to the next level, but doing the opposite—bringing on the wrong ones at the wrong time—can have a disastrous impact on the business and the entrepreneur. To make the right choice for your company, you should understand both the opportunities and the limitations that come with assembling a team.

Before you can begin building your team, you must ask yourself those five famous "W" questions: Who, What, Where, When, and Why. Let's take each question one by one.

WHO *exactly* are you looking to hire?

This may sound like a basic question, but many entrepreneurs forget to give it thorough consideration. What kind of person would be ideal for the role? What experience does he have, and what skills must she possess to excel in the position? What are you willing to compromise on, and what are your deal breakers? Whether you're searching for an assistant, associate, or executive-level employee, it's important to fine-tune your expectations before the search begins.

If the goal is to hire a team that rounds out your skill set, you may find it helpful to revisit Chapter Two—where you were asked to identify your strengths and weaknesses. Or perhaps you're looking to bring on people who can directly affect the bottom line. When Barbara Corcoran was first building the Corcoran Group, she put every extra penny toward hiring sales associates. She knew that the only way to grow the company was to build the sales force, so she focused all her efforts on that.

Write out a short (one page) document describing the kind of person you're looking to hire, and be sure to get as specific as possible. Whatever you do, try to avoid the dreaded "I'll know it when I see it" approach. If you don't know it, you're pretty much guaranteed to never see it.

WHAT expectations do you have for the role(s)?

From administrative duties to high-level tasks, small business owners are used to wearing many hats. They often look for someone who can do a little bit of everything. From the entrepreneur's perspective it just makes sense: "My role is vast and never-ending, why shouldn't my employees have the same experience?" Well, because it's not *their* company.

From your very first hire, you should set clear objectives for every role. If you bring on an accountant, for instance, you can't expect that person to also be responsible for building the brand, generating leads, and sweeping the floor. It's possible that you may be able to find someone who will do all that, but he's likely to be less proficient at his accounting duties.

While most people who choose to work for a startup anticipate a less-structured environment, it's your job to help your employees succeed. And the only way to do that is to provide a framework for success.

WHERE will you find your employee?

Once you have a good idea of the kind of person you're looking to attract and the role you'd like to build, next you'll need to actually go about finding the right candidate. While there are plenty of services to help with the job search, most often your best tool is your network.

Whether you know it or not, it's likely you're a mere one or two degrees away from your dream hire. Before you begin posting ads online or using a recruiter, do a little investigation into people you might already have in your network. LinkedIn can be a great resource for this type of discovery, but you shouldn't feel limited to just one social network. Create a special page on your website that details the opportunity and post it on Facebook, Twitter, or Google Plus. You never know which friend of a friend might stumble across the opportunity and decide to apply.

WHEN is the best time to make the hire?

You may want an employee this month, but that doesn't mean it's necessarily the best time to hire. When you begin building a team, you take on many new responsibilities, both financially and operationally. Depending on how you choose to structure the role, you may need to pay additional taxes, buy insurance, or make other financial adjustments. In fact, it's usually best to consult your accountant or lawyer before beginning the process, as laws differ from state to state.

You must also consider that when you bring on an employee you're now more than just an entrepreneur; you're a manager as well. Outside of just basic training, it'll be up to you to manage your employees, which of course creates additional work. Therefore, it's best to approach hiring, especially at the beginning, from a strategic perspective—instead of just based on your immediate needs. Knowing when to bring on an employee is sometimes just as important as the employee herself.

WHY are you looking to build your team?

Identifying the "why" behind a decision is often the most challenging part of any process. But it's also usually the most revealing and rewarding. Why exactly are you looking to begin building your team now? Have you experienced rapid growth? Are you feeling overwhelmed and eager to offload some extra responsibilities? Are you trying to legitimize a struggling business? While some of these reasons are obviously better than others, it's crucial that you explore yours. This reflection will ensure that you're making the right decision to bring on a team.

SHARK BITE

"When you hire an employee you have to realize he is not your friend; he is there to execute the business plan at that particular time. And as the business changes, so too will the specific skill sets you require. I expect a lot of turnover in businesses that are successful."

KEVIN

Only once you're able to answer the five W's will the "how" slowly begin to reveal itself. And, of course, once it does you'll be faced with a whole new set of challenges to tackle and decisions to make.

INDEPENDENT CONTRACTOR VS. EMPLOYEE

For most businesses, the hiring process looks very different than it did even ten years ago. Today it's possible to run an entire company remotely—with employees based in different states, or sometimes even different countries. In short, the days of having one team under one roof are quickly fading and making room for new ways of doing business.

As the professional landscape shifts and grows, so too do the roles of the employee and the entrepreneur. No longer interested in *only* hiring full-time employees, It's common for companies to bring on independent contractors (or freelancers) to fill critical roles.

An independent contractor is defined as "a person who contracts to do work for another person according to his or her own processes and methods." Writers, accountants, and lawyers are all good examples of traditional independent contractor roles, but the job category is quickly expanding. From design to support services, more than 17 million Americans work as independent contractors each year—a number that's expected to hit 23 million by 2017. And while this blossoming role has its own set of obstacles for business owners to consider, it often provides a great alternative for entrepreneurs looking to save money and decrease liabilities.

When you hire a contractor, as opposed to a full-time employee, you are not required to withhold income taxes or pay

SHARK BITE

"When it comes to hiring, the most important thing is that you just go out and do it—even if you think you're only 50 percent ready—because it forces you to grow your business. Immediately you have a problem, you have a deadline, you have to grow it. And there's nothing better than a deadline. It always works."

BARBARA

Social Security, Medicare, or unemployment tax. You are also void of certain types of liabilities and not required to pay benefits of any sort. But before you decide to rethink your hiring strategy and work only with contractors, keep in mind that this role has its limitations.

A freelancer has the right to accept or deny any project he chooses. In other words, the independent contractor always retains complete control of her work life. So even though working with independent contractors may bring down your hiring costs significantly, it may also create challenges you're unwilling to deal with. Most likely, it will be a good solution for some roles and less ideal for others.

ATTRACTING GREAT PEOPLE

The individuals you choose to hire are the lifeblood of your organization. Not only are they the people you'll be spending the majority of your time with, they are also the face of your company—an extension of your brand. Whether you're looking to bring on a full-time employee or simply work with an independent contractor, you'll want to attract the highest-caliber candidate possible. Therefore, you will first need to make some key decisions about what type of compensation package you can offer and how you'll position the opportunity.

Outbidding the competition isn't the only way to secure great employees. Believe it or not, just the fact that you're a startup can be a great competitive advantage, as many people are drawn to the energy and opportunity a new venture offers. In fact, being able to provide a unique and purposeful work experience can often be your greatest selling point. Below are a few additional strategies you can utilize to attract great people.

Get creative with the job title: What's in a name, you ask? Both everything and nothing at all. One of the benefits of building a company from the ground up is that there isn't a lot of pesky infrastructure or obnoxious red tape to get in the way. While this can occasionally create an overall lack of structure, it also leaves room for tremendous freedom.

Although you most likely won't be able to match the compensation package of a larger, more established company, what you lack in funds you can certainly make up for in creativity, especially when it comes to job titles. If you're hiring a sales associate, for instance, and you can only afford to pay 70 percent of what other companies are offering, you may wish to sweeten the deal by repositioning the role as "senior sales director." What do you care? An upgraded title doesn't mean much to you at all. But it can make the employee feel more valued and help him secure a better job in the future.

Don't let titles get in your way. Use them as bargaining chips to secre higher-caliber employees.

Load up on the perks: During the startup phase, it's common to work long hours for little pay. One of the best ways to offset this pain is to offer your employees valuable perks. From free daily lunch and laundry drop-off service to regular outings and complimentary gym memberships, many startups have found great success by offering employees small, but thoughtful extras.

But won't people just do the math and realize that a free gym membership isn't worth $10,000 less in annual salary? Maybe, but that's not necessarily the point. Plenty of studies suggest that money isn't always the determining factor when people seek a new position, especially for the younger generations. Offering small perks can be a good way to stand out and show that you appreciate your employees. Even if you own a very small company, there are many ways of getting group rates for local services. You may find it advantageous to partner with other local business owners to secure better deals. The more people you have on your side, the better poised you'll be to negotiate.

Provide professional development opportunities: Today's workers are not looking for a static opportunity; they want a position that has the potential to grow and evolve with them. Likewise, they want to feel challenged and inspired by their work. An easy and relatively low-cost way to empower your employees to excel is to provide complimentary professional development opportunities. Whether that's by offering scholarships to local education programs, hosting your own unique learning event, or bringing in an expert to work one-on-one, showing that you're invested in the overall professional development of your team is a great way to let employees know you value their dedication and service.

While each of these can be effective strategies for enticing new hires, your greatest asset is something far more important than a few scattered perks or learning opportunities. It's the DNA of your organization, your corporate fingerprint; it is your culture.

TANK TIP

"You've got to know how to identify strengths and weaknesses in others. But even more importantly, you must learn how to recognize skilled people and plug them into your life and business. Surrounding yourself with talented, quality people is the best way to find true success"

—RICK HOPPER, FOUNDER OF READEREST

CREATING KILLER CULTURE

If this book were your company, then its binding would be your culture, because in many ways that's what culture does: it pieces together the various fragments of an organization into one dynamic tapestry that represents your business.

From your office space to communication strategy, culture dictates how you'll run your business and, in many cases, can be the deciding factor for a new hire. Think about it: the average person spends more than a quarter of her life at work. Double (or triple!) that for entrepreneurs. Of course it makes sense for someone to choose a culture that matches his values.

And this is great news for small business owners because it provides yet another opportunity to be competitive. Let's say, for example, that Candidate A has a job offer from a big corporation that's willing to pay $100,000 a year plus benefits. Your company on the other hand can only afford to pay $75,000 a year with limited benefits. On paper it makes sense for Candidate A to go with the big corporation. She'd be making 25 percent more money annually and have a better all-around package. But remember, there's more to the decision than just salary. If Candidate A is more attracted to your culture and feels as though your business would be a better place to work, it's very possible that your offer may be the more attractive one.

Since culture can be a powerful differentiator, it makes sense to build one that embodies your brand and champions your mission. Here are three primary areas to focus on when building or improving your culture:

Employees: How does it feel to work for your company? This can be a difficult question to answer, mainly because it requires you to take an honest look at the inner workings of your organization. Do you give your team flexibility and freedom, or do you insist on a more controlled environment? Are your employees regularly empowered to make important decisions, or must they adapt to a more hierarchical, top-down system?

Every great culture is rooted in people, so it's important to put yourself in your team's shoes. Would you like working for your company if you weren't the boss? If you answered no, you may want to begin rethinking your approach. By building a superb culture, you improve the lives of your employees, and you better believe that satisfaction extends to your customers as well.

Environment: What's the best way to boost both productivity and creativity? For many companies, the solution lies in creating a more productive environment.

If you champion the free flow of ideas, it doesn't make much sense for you and your employees to sit in a large room full of cubicles. If you believe in building a democratic organization where leadership and employees work in tandem, you may wish to rethink a floor plan that puts employees in their own sequestered offices. If your environment is working against culture, brainstorm with your team and come up with a few creative ways to reimagine your space. Believe it or not, the environment you create can play a distinct role in your culture and business.

Impact: Customers and employees are the secret to your business's success, but zoom out for a moment and consider the bigger question: How does your business impact the community? And what does that impact say about you as a company? Are you a beacon of responsibility? A steward of progress? Maybe that's not the appropriate image for your brand. Perhaps your company is about promoting fun or advocating independence. Your impact is more than just part of your brand; it's a significant part of your culture.

To understand this idea more completely, try to examine the topic through the lens of *Shark Tank*. Assume for a moment that each Shark is not a person, but a company. If Kevin O'Leary was Kevin O'Leary, Inc., what kind of expectations would you have about the company's products or services? What kind of people might they hire? How might you imagine they would go about doing business? Now compare that to Robert Herjavec, Inc. or Lori Greiner, Inc.? Whether you want it to or not, the impact you have on the outside world

"Culture will half determine your business's success. If it's good, it creates an environment that brings out and attracts the best people. If it's not good, sadly, it will repel the best people. As an entrepreneur, it's up to you to be a walking, talking example of your culture. It's a crucial part of running a business and something that most small business owners don't spend enough time thinking about."

BARBARA

seeps into your organization and becomes a signature part of your culture.

If you want your company to grow and flourish, if you wish to attract the most talented employees and the most loyal customers, you must work to create a culture that represents your business's point of view. It won't happen overnight, but ask anyone who's put the time and energy into building a prosperous culture, and they'll most likely agree: it's worth the effort.

GOODBYE, AND GOOD LUCK: FIRING WITH DIGNITY

Nobody enjoys having to fire an employee. However, there will likely come a time when you're tasked with the unsavory deed. Although it is never a comfortable or enjoyable process, there are ways to soften the blow and make it more tolerable for both parties. Below is a list of common dos and don'ts to consider before terminating an employee:

DO be brief and to the point: Sugarcoating is for candy, not for firing. Think of the classic Band-Aid example: a swift rip is far better than a slow and drawn-out tear. Skip the pleasantries and immediately get to the issue at hand.

DO NOT fire anyone over the phone: Even if your employee works primarily from home, this is a conversation you'll want to have in person. If for any reason the employee can't make it the office, try to find a neutral and private third location for the meeting.

DO have data to support the decision: In many states you do not need a specific reason to terminate an employee, but you still want to make sure you have solid data to back up your decision. For one, it will be helpful to let the employee know what he did wrong. But you'll also want to be prepared should the employee choose to take litigious action.

DO NOT change your mind: Think long and hard about the decision before firing anyone. You should never change your mind mid-meeting or let the employee believe there's any chance for rebuttal. You must be confident and firm in your decision and delivery.

DO be discreet and private: Because of the sensitivity of the issue you should strive to be as discreet and private as possible when letting someone go. Even if emotions are high, allow cooler heads to prevail, and act with the highest possible level of respect and integrity.

DO NOT fire anyone alone: While you should try to be as

discreet as possible, it's important that someone else is present when the termination is taking place. If you don't have any other senior level employees, you may wish to bring your lawyer or accountant into the meeting.

DO have a follow-up plan: No matter the role of the person you terminate, there will likely be some sort of operational fallout to the employee leaving. Make sure you have a plan in place to deal with the extra workload and any cultural upsets that may need mending.

DO NOT let the word get out: Under no circumstances should you let word get out in advance. Getting fired is a touchy subject, and you should do everything in your power to minimize the discomfort for everyone on your team.

Before you initiate any termination, make sure you're legally prepared for any potential fallout. Chances are slim that an employee will try to sue, but it's a good idea to triple-check that you've taken all the necessary precautions. Although the firing process is difficult, sometimes it's the only way to move forward and build a better organization.

13

LEADING THE CHARGE

I f you're an accountant, it's likely your role is fairly easy to define: inspect and maintain financial records. If you're a barista, you probably have a good sense of your general responsibilities: make delicious caffeinated beverages for thirsty consumers. But if you were to ask a room full of entrepreneurs to describe, in one sentence, the entirety of their roles and responsibilities, you would receive, at the very best, a hearty laugh.

If your business is growing and evolving, it only makes sense that your role as an entrepreneur will grow and evolve as well. While you may have spent the first phase developing a product or service, eventually the task will be complete. At that point, your day-to-day routine will be less about innovation and creation and more about long-term strategy and management. For some entrepreneurs this will be a welcome change; for others it will be more challenging.

Depending on your specific business, you may find yourself leading a team of two or a team of two hundred. Regardless of your team's size, leadership must always be rooted in purpose. An accidental leader is no leader at all.

SHARK BITE

"Being a good leader isn't about providing social mentoring or being Dr. Phil. It's about communicating the business goals to everyone from the CEO to the secretary and explaining how those goals will be achieved."

KEVIN

The subject of leadership is a complex and highly charged one, with an ever-expanding set of rules and philosophies. Scour the business section of any bookstore and you'll find stacks of titles on the subject. Inquire online and you'll discover even more material—a simple search for the term "business leadership" returns over 3 million results. With so much information available on the topic, it's almost guaranteed that one philosophy will contradict the next.

What you must always remember is that there isn't one way to lead. In other words, it's not a matter of right or wrong, but of more effective versus less effective. While some choose to adopt a more participatory, open style of leadership, others favor a more structured, rigid approach. And that's okay; there's room for both. As the leader of your company, it's *you* who must decide how to steer the ship, and what kind of captain you'll be.

A NEW GENERATION OF LEADERSHIP

Before you define your role as a leader, you must first understand the role of the employee, which has dramatically changed over the last couple of decades. Fifty years ago most people dreamed of graduating from college, getting a well-paying job at a reputable company, and climbing the corporate ladder until they could eventually retire and collect a pension. But the days of such a well-defined path to success are over. Today, people are searching for more than just a j-o-b; they want opportunity that feels deeply meaningful and uniquely their own. Perhaps that very desire was your initial motivation for starting a business.

As cultural expectations surrounding work have evolved, so too has the role of the leader. Top-down management and rigid structure just aren't as effective as they once were. The days of corporate authoritarianism are rapidly coming to an end and making room for a new generation of leadership—one that isn't as much about power and assertion as it is about influence and inspiration. Being a good leader today is not about how obsessively you can control, but how abundantly you can empower.

So what does that mean for you—the entrepreneur, the small business owner? How do you excel as a leader? While this subject is expansive, there are four distinct principles that can be applied to almost every type of leadership: Authenticity, Adaptability, Accountability, and Accessibility.

Authenticity: Just as consumers are demanding more authenticity and transparency from the businesses they support, employees are looking to leadership for the same. As a leader you needn't have all the right answers. Instead, it's far more important that a leader is genuine in his messaging and honest about his strengths and weaknesses. Your team is your team for a reason. They don't just believe in your business; they believe in you as well. Reward that trust and respect with a commitment to lead authentically—even when it's the tough choice to make.

Adaptability: We live in a constantly evolving society where disruption occurs in greater, more pervasive ways than ever before. What works today may very well not work next year. An integral part of being a good leader is knowing how to stay nimble and adaptable. No, of course you should never sway from your core values and mission. Without those, your organization would be lost. But you also cannot be rigid or stagnant in the face of change. One size no longer fits all, and it's up to you to create a system that embraces change.

Accountability: There's a school of leadership out there that says you must stand tall, act proud, and never admit wrongdoing, for fear of being seen as weak or vulnerable. That is the school of the past, not of the future. Today's leaders must be unapologetically accountable for all their decisions—the good and the bad. You need only look to pop culture to find proof of this principle. What's the worst thing celebrities, politicians, or business leaders can do when they make a public blunder? Deflect blame. Although the initial desire may be to point fingers or deny responsibility, that choice only results in more turmoil. It may seem backwards, but when you admit you were wrong and show real accountability, you humanize the leadership role. In doing so, you draw people *closer* to you and your organization. You will make mistakes. That's a guarantee. And when you do, you must be strong enough to take full accountability for your actions. Otherwise, your leadership may only be temporary.

Accessibility: In some circles there's still a stigma about being too accessible. If everyone can reach you, what does it say about your status or clout? But being inaccessible isn't a sign of power; it's a sign of being out of touch. As a society we have become accustomed to immediate feedback. Thanks to communication platforms like social media, email, and text messages, unlimited accessibility is now the rule, not the exception. Most employees, for instance, don't want to wait six months for a formal review to see how they're performing. They want access to information now. And it's not just access to information they want; it's access to leadership too. Politicians are expected to embrace social media; corporate titans are encouraged to blog. Being a leader in today's world means embracing accessibility both from a philosophical and an operational point of view.

When you examine these four principles, you begin to notice they all have one fascinating thing in common. These are all qualities that one typically expects from *personal* relationships. Everybody wants friends who are authentic and adaptable, right? Who wouldn't want their loved ones to be accountable and accessible?

For years, personal and professional expectations have been independent of one another, but slowly they're beginning to merge. As the line between work and life continues to blur, so too do our expectations of each. When you begin to understand this idea, when you begin to recognize that the chasm between personal and professional is narrowing, the more these principles start to make sense. This isn't a generational shift. This isn't a trend. What we are witnessing is the beginning of a new way of working and a new era of leadership.

WHAT KIND OF LEADER ARE YOU?

When assessing your company and considering your role as a leader, it's natural to use other companies or individuals as inspiration: "I want to be like Richard Branson" or "I want my company to run like Nike." Identifying these types of

SHARK BITE

"I'm not much of a leader, so I try to hire great people who are and who can get the job done."

MARK

examples may be a helpful starting point, but it should only be the beginning of your journey.

Being a great leader isn't a prix fixe meal that can just be ordered up (e.g., "I'll have what he's having."). Rather, leadership is more of a buffet. And as with a buffet, you must exercise the discipline and discernment to take what you need and leave the rest behind. Otherwise, your plate will become far too crowded and overwhelming.

If you asked the President of the United States or the CEO of a major corporation to define his leadership style, he probably wouldn't give you a clear-cut answer. When you're a leader, you're a leader, not a specific *type* of leader. So, while it isn't always necessary to commit to any one leadership style, it's helpful to know which ones are most effective for achieving certain types of results.

Below you'll find seven of the most common leadership styles. Which ones are the best fit for you and your organization? Again, this isn't about picking one and leaving the rest behind. The goal should be to explore the various approaches and cultivate your own unique approach.

Democratic: The democratic leader takes a more collective approach to the decision making process. Instead of one person or one group of people making all the major decisions, she asks the larger group to participate. This type of leadership has been proven to be highly effective, as it helps employees feel more involved in the company. However, it does also have its drawbacks. Democratic leadership has been known to create unnecessary confusion within the organization, which often leads to poor communication and disorganization. IDEAL FOR: a smaller organization that has a team of employees with equal skill levels.

Authoritarian: When most people imagine the leader-follower relationship, authoritarian (or autocratic) leadership may be the first thing that comes to mind. Leaders who subscribe to this method typically make decisions on their own. If you've ever had a controlling boss who takes pleasure in micromanaging your work, than you may already be familiar with this type of leadership. But don't discount it just yet. Not all authoritarian leaders abuse their power or become ruthless dictators; autocracy is more of a spectrum than a single shade. IDEAL FOR: an organization where the boss may have considerably more knowledge than the rest of the team or if decision-making must often occur quickly.

Transformational: Transformational leaders are often big thinkers and even bigger talkers. They're known for their ability to inspire and motivate others to perform. Often characterized by their enthusiasm and passion, they genuinely see the best in others and put attitude above almost everything else. While this type of leader can do a lot for an organization, it's important that detail-oriented and analytical people support him. Otherwise, this leader's grand visions may never be more than just that: visions. IDEAL FOR: an organization where innovation is crucial to success.

Laissez-faire: As its name suggests, this type of leader is by far the most hands-off, asking each team member to make her own decisions while simultaneously providing little guidance. Because its very definition requires a substantial amount of passivity, studies have shown that this is one of the least effective ways to lead a team and manage a business. IDEAL FOR: an organization with a small group of high-performing experts.

Servant: First identified by Robert Greenleaf, this type of leadership is centered on helping others live up to their fullest potential. A servant leader will often share power and put a significant effort into her team members' professional development. Different from democratic leadership, there is still a primary management team in place. However, much of their responsibility is empowering those within the organization to grow and flourish. This leadership style has dramatically grown in popularity over the last ten or fifteen years. IDEAL FOR: organizations with a well-organized, mission-focused leadership team.

Transactional: Working under the primary belief that employees should be rewarded or punished based on performance, this type of leader values organization, structure, and a solidified chain of command. Furthermore, a transactional leader takes great comfort in rules, process, and procedure, and expects others to do the same. When business is going well and performance is high, this type of leader is often beloved. But when things start to go downhill, watch out! The transactional leader believes in swift but firm penalization for errors and oversights. More effective for certain types of teams than others, transactional leadership can have both a positive and negative effect on an organization. IDEAL FOR: traditional organizations with a robust team of middle management.

Affiliative: The affiliative leader believes more than anything else that people come first. Often prioritizing emotions over

"I don't like to micromanage. I believe in the people I hire, and so I respect the decisions they make."

DAYMOND

performance, everything this type of leader does is designed to provide comfort and harmony for the team. Therefore, most of his time and energy is spent focusing on connection and collaboration. While this type of leader can offer value to an organization, a natural aversion to conflict often stands in her way. IDEAL FOR: an organization looking to improve culture and strengthen morale.

Identifying what type(s) of leadership you wish to adopt can have an extraordinary impact on your business. For one, it will greatly determine whom you choose to work with (and who chooses to work with you). But it will also provide you with a basic outline and game plan for how to effectively lead your team. Take a moment to consider which type of leadership speaks to you.

SHARING THE LOAD

No matter which leadership style you choose to adopt, one thing is certain: you *must* learn how to delegate responsibility. For many entrepreneurs, this can feel like an impossible task. After they've spent so much time building, creating, and growing an organization, it's difficult to hand over even the smallest amount of control. But knowing when and how to delegate is a crucial part of becoming a great leader.

To do this successfully, first, you have to get over the common misconception that a leader must always maintain complete control. From revenue to staffing, many believe that leadership means you have to be in charge . . . of everything. But of course you know that isn't true. While a good leader must be responsible for laying out the vision, he needn't execute every part of the process.

Earlier in the book you were asked to identify your strengths and weaknesses. No matter how talented or exceptional you are, it's likely your list of weaknesses will rival your list of strengths. That's a good thing. By being aware of your deficits, you can begin to delegate appropriate tasks and focus only on the things you do well.

Delegation is challenging for everyone—even for someone as successful as the Sharks. "I have learned to delegate," writes Mark Cuban on his blog. "That's not easy for an entrepreneur to do. In my past, I would have taken on everything and anything I thought could add value to. I had to be in the middle of everything. No longer. I've learned to hire people that I can build trust in and let them take the ball and run with it."

Delegation isn't just good for you; it's good for the company as a whole. When you delegate a task, you're essentially giving someone your vote. You're saying, "I believe you can do this well." This proof of confidence boosts morale and encourages a culture of initiation and trust—something that every organization can appreciate.

If you have difficulty delegating, begin by taking baby steps. Don't turn over all your financials to someone just yet. Start small. Assign a task that won't make or break the organization, and give the subordinate a chance to figure it out on her own. As you begin to see your team excel at new tasks, it's likely you'll grow more comfortable with the idea of handing

SHARK BITE

"Delegation can be very difficult for the entrepreneur. It's hard to let go. Personally, I try to hire smart people whom I like, trust, and admire. And then I spend a lot of time communicating the big picture of my company's mission. Most entrepreneurs don't start out being great at delegation; they have to learn as they go."

LORI

off some of the larger ones. After a while, you'll see just how much time you free up—time you can use to grow the company and focus on the larger vision.

There's a famous Buddhist expression that says, "Thousands of candles can be lighted from a single candle, and the life of the candle will not be shortened." The same is true for delegation. You never lose power by empowering others. Quite the opposite in fact. The very best leaders know when to lead and when to stand back and let others take the reins.

YOUR RIGHT HAND:
HIRING A GREAT MANAGER

Not every entrepreneur is a good manager and not every manager is a good entrepreneur. As a leader, it's up to you to decide whether or not you're the best person to handle the day-to-day operations of your company.

Many entrepreneurs are attracted to the building process—taking an organization from idea to reality. But when it comes to actually running the company, they're bored out of their minds. If you're this type of person, it may be helpful to bring on an outside manager to help run the business.

When hiring a manager, it's common for entrepreneurs to look for someone like themselves: daring, bold, and perhaps a little untraditional. But bringing on a carbon copy of yourself may not be the best thing for your business. As you learned in the previous chapter, you want to hire someone who rounds out your skill set. When looking for a good manager, it's best to step back and think about what your organization really needs to advance to the next level. Are you terrible at organization? Then bringing on a manager who is a hyper-organizer is a smart idea. Are you a notoriously big-picture thinker? That will serve your organization well, but only when fused with a more logistical and operational mind.

The greatest challenge most entrepreneurs face when hiring a manager is that the process requires a healthy dose of self-assessment. Some business owners, especially those who are self-made, can be judgmental of those who have taken a more traditional route. To them, such a path seems unthinkable. But this is a bias you simply can't afford to have. Formalized experience can be a great thing, especially when combined with the gutsy bravado that a homegrown entrepreneur brings to the table. Although you may find a few philosophical differences in your respective approaches, it's likely your combined experience will make for an all-around better organization.

When you're hiring a manager to help lead your business, it's okay to bring on someone with more work experience than yourself—even if it slightly bruises your pride. Having someone on board with real-world experience in a similar industry can help your company avoid common pitfalls and ultimately save you time and money. Think of it like having a corporate tour guide on staff.

It's your job as a leader to build the best business you can, and occasionally that may mean turning over some of the leadership responsibilities to someone else. Don't be afraid to ask yourself the tough question, "Am I the right person to run this company?" You may be surprised to see just how transformational the answer can be.

14

THE SMART WAY TO GROW

Whenever the words "growth" and "business" are combined, people start to get excited—especially if the business in question is their own. But growth is a complicated thing, with many positive and negative implications. While growth usually means more profit, it can also mean a complete revision of the company, which can be a time-consuming and expensive task.

Before you can properly craft a growth strategy, you must first identify what ideal growth looks like for *your* company. Not all small businesses will grow or should grow the same way, and bigger doesn't necessarily mean better. Everyone has an opinion on how and when to expand, but one thing is universally true: you must have some sort of growth plan.

"Too many small business don't have a plan for growth," says Robert Herjavec. "Even when my company was small and just starting out, we always had a target for what we were going to do each year. People are afraid to put a plan together because they feel it makes them accountable, and it does."

As you begin to think about your growth strategy, you'll

want to be sure you have all the right pieces in place. Otherwise, you could end up growing too fast or too soon (yes, there's such a thing as both!). Before taking any major steps toward expansion, be sure to answer the following questions:

Do you have access to enough capital?

It *takes* money to *make* money, and this is particularly true during any period of significant growth. Even if you have enough capital to start a business, any sort of significant growth will most likely require an infusion of additional money. According to leaders at the Small Business Administration, "The biggest challenge facing small businesses right now is that too many good, creditworthy borrowers still can't find the capital they need to grow and create jobs." In other words, if you don't have access to capital, you may find yourself stuck in one place.

Let's say, for example, that you own a toy company, and you've just received a massive purchase order from a big-box retailer. That can be a tremendous opportunity for your business, but only if you can deliver. An order that triples your output means you'll need triple the funds to produce the goods, which can be a cumbersome expense.

In Chapter Seven you learned the importance of managing your cash flow and staying on top of your financials. This is absolutely crucial when you're attempting to grow. The very worst-case scenario is that you lose out on an incredible deal because you didn't have the capital in place to see it through.

Have you built the necessary infrastructure?

Imagine that you own a small artisanal chocolate company. You've spent years slowly building the business and creating a high-quality, handmade product that your customers absolutely love. You are the very best chocolate company in town and have a devoted base of loyal fans. Then one day, quite by accident, the editor of a high-volume magazine receives a box of your chocolates. She loves them so much that she decides to do a big story about your company in her publication. The story does well, and you get twenty times the amount of orders you've ever received. Sounds like what dreams are made of, right? Maybe, but also maybe not.

All of a sudden your quaint little artisanal chocolate shop is faced with a major challenge. How do you keep up with volume while still maintaining the integrity of the product? In order to do so, you must have the proper infrastructure and materials in place to handle such growth. It's likely you'll need more machines, a bigger kitchen, and perhaps even a new fulfillment center. But it doesn't stop there. As a chocolate maker, you rely on your vendors. What does growth look like across the supply chain? Will you have access to the same quality cacao and sugar? If not, how will that affect your product?

Growing a business can be thrilling or terrifying, and often it's a little bit of both. If you want to ensure that your growth is sustainable, you must consider both your infrastructure and materials before trying to expand.

Do you have the manpower to pull it off?

In the previous two chapters you learned how to build a great team and get comfortable with the delegation process. Those skills will serve you especially well when trying to grow.

Going back to the chocolate company example, not only would you need to have the necessary infrastructure in place, but you would also need the workers to keep up with the influx of orders. If you have to hire fast, chances are you aren't going to find the best people for the jobs, so it's important to be prepared from the outset.

There may be some situations where growth happens organically or by sheer accident. In those cases, you'll just have to think on your feet. But more often than not, growth isn't accidental; it's a calculated and strategic move. Many of the entrepreneurs who appear on *Shark Tank*, for instance, know that they'll experience a surge of growth once their episode airs on television. Therefore it would be in their best interest to secure the necessary employees in advance.

Depending on the type of expected growth, you may wish to bring on freelancers, hourly workers, or full-time employees. That's up to you. But no matter which type of employee you hire, be sure that you have some sort of plan in place. There are only twenty-four hours in any given day, and you have to sleep for at least . . . two or three of those.

Does your growth strategy align with your overall mission and vision?
Many believe that money can change a person. Well, if it can change a person, it can definitely change a business. One of the most common hurdles an entrepreneur encounters when experiencing growth is maintaining the mission and vision of the organization.

As more opportunities begin to arise, naturally things start to get more complicated. The chocolate company, for example, built their business on a handmade, artisanal product. If they experience rapid growth and don't have access to the same quality of materials, all of a sudden the very core principles of their business are in danger. Now they must make a difficult choice: do they refine the mission to accommodate growth or do they stay true to the original vision and ignore opportunity? That's a tough one. While there's nothing wrong with altering the fundamentals of a business, you must be aware of the effect it can have on the organization as a whole.

When your business makes a promise (e.g., handmade, artisanal chocolate), you sign an unofficial contract with the customer. When that promise is revised, so too is the contract, which could jeopardize your entire base.

Growth can be a magical and intoxicating thing. There's nothing like watching something that was once just an idea transform into a beloved product or service. But too much growth at the wrong time can hurt, or worse, destroy a business. As you begin to experience growth, it's a good idea to go back and review your original business plan. Update your market research, revisit your mission, and perform an in-depth analysis on your financials. Use this as an opportunity to refresh your goals and refocus your positioning.

What's the current state of your brand? Where are you succeeding and where are you failing? Which marketing efforts are working and which are a waste of time? How do your sales match up to your projections? As you begin to revisit these crucial questions you may discover areas of growth that you never considered or hurdles that you didn't know were even there. You might learn that you need to pay better attention to how you measure success. Perhaps you'll find a

SHARK BITE

"The idea that growth equals profitability is a misconception. If you can't afford the financial or qualitative side of growth, it can just as easily put you out of business. You must have the money to provide your customers with what they need, when they need it."

MARK

new piece of technology that can greatly improve the efficiency of your operations. The more intel you can gather, the better off you'll be.

Remember, growth is specific to your organization, and you must treat it as such. As an entrepreneur, it's up to you not only to carve the path but also to lead the way. And that requires knowing where you came from and where you're headed.

FRANCHISING YOUR BUSINESS

What's the fastest way to grow a company and turn it into a household name? For some businesses, the answer may lie in franchising. In the first part of this book you learned the pros and cons of *purchasing* a franchise, but that's only one side of the coin. From an ownership perspective, the franchise business looks entirely different.

As you might imagine, becoming a franchisor is a lengthy and often complicated process that requires an abundance of not only patience but also money. Between up-front and operational costs, the price of franchising a business can range from tens of thousands to hundreds of thousands of dollars. It all depends on how you choose to go about the process. Keep in mind, however, that most first-time franchisors will require the help of consultants and lawyers, which can considerably rack up the price, so it's always best to budget a little more than you think. But even though the initial costs can be hefty, franchising a business can be incredibly lucrative.

The U.S. Census Bureau reported that in 2007, franchises made up 10.5 percent of businesses across 295 industries. In total, those franchises accounted for $1.3 trillion in revenue and the creation of 7.9 million jobs. Sound too good to be true? The next time you drive down a highway, try to count the number of franchises you spot. From fast-food restaurants and gas stations to specialty stores and even law firms, franchises are more prevalent than you might imagine.

Still, don't let that $1.3 trillion number blind you; not every great company makes a great franchise. Before saving up for your big franchise rollout, pause for a moment and carefully evaluate whether it's the right decision for your particular business.

The primary issue to consider is the market size of your business. Most often, the franchises that work the best have a huge market and appeal to a broad spectrum of consumers. If, for instance, you own an antique yo-yo store that specializes in hand-engraved yo-yo accessories (if there even is such a thing), then franchising your business may not be the best growth strategy. The specialty engraved yo-yo accessories market just isn't that large. On the other hand, if you own a quick-service salad restaurant with a strong brand identity and a unique twist, then franchising may be an option worth considering.

One of the best ways to identify whether your concept is fit for franchising is to put it through the "mall test." Would your business succeed inside (or around) any mall in America? While this test won't apply across the board, it's often a quick way to determine whether your business has real franchise potential. After you've done the mall test on your business, try it out on other proven franchises, like for instance any of the top ten companies on *Entrepreneur* magazine's 2013 Franchise 500 list:

1. Hampton Hotels
2. Subway
3. Jiffy Lube International, Inc.

4. 7-Eleven, Inc.
5. Supercuts
6. Anytime Fitness
7. Servpro
8. Denny's, Inc.
9. McDonald's
10. Pizza Hut, Inc.

More telling than the actual businesses, play close attention to the categories: restaurant, hotel, auto repair, salon, gym, convenience store, and cleanup service. Excluding Servpro, the cleanup and disaster repair company, each of these businesses would perform remarkably well inside or around just about any mall in America.

Of course you must also think about whether or not your business will fit within the more rigid confines of a franchise structure. Part of the reason people purchase a franchise is for the ease that comes with running a more plug-and-play style of business. From store design and pricing to training and marketing, the franchisee is buying more than just the business; he's buying the model as well. This means that before you can even think about franchising, you must have a fully developed infrastructure. Do you have a reliable network of vendors? Have you come up with a proven marketing strategy? Do you have a training program in place? Do you have someone on your team who will be designated to handle franchisee relationships? Without the necessary elements, it may be difficult to sell your franchise.

According to the International Franchise Association, more than 40 of the 105 companies that began selling franchises in 2008 had yet to report their first sale by the end of 2009. That's almost half. This statistic shows just how difficult it can be to

SHARK BITE

"Before any business can franchise they need the two magic ingredients. First is an ironclad and tested model that can be replicated. And the second is a franchisee who is so excited about the business he can't help but tell the world how great it is. It's only when you have both of those elements that a franchise can really take off."

BARBARA

sell a new franchise. And when you think about it, it makes perfect sense. Why would a franchisee buy your business when they could purchase one that's already proven? Will you offer lower fees? A better supply chain? More rewards and benefits? As part of your preparation you must determine how your business will differentiate itself in the crowded franchise market.

For some businesses, franchising can be a wonderful way to grow, especially if the money and resources are in place. However, as with any large strategic move, you should plan for success but prepare for failure. Otherwise your franchise could end up becoming just another statistic.

SELLING YOUR BUSINESS

While many entrepreneurs will start a venture with dreams of an eventual sale, the majority of small business owners haven't given the subject much thought. But whether or not you have a finely crafted exit strategy, at some point you may want to consider selling your company.

Not only can selling your business be a difficult professional decision, it can be an emotionally challenging one as well. As you've learned throughout this book, building a business is an intense process that requires considerable time, effort, and care. Letting go of something that you've invested so much of yourself in can feel overwhelming. Still, selling your business may be the right move, especially if a desirable and profitable opportunity presents itself at the right time. And that's exactly what it often comes down to: timing.

What's trendy and desirable one year may very well be irrelevant the next. Conversely, it's possible for an entire industry to experience a sudden burst of growth, making a relatively unknown business extremely popular. As a business owner, it's important for you to acknowledge the role of timing in your decision to sell—both from a business and a personal perspective. Are you really ready to walk away? Do you have a game plan in place for what's next? Before making the decision to sell, research the industry. Where are things headed? Is it likely your business will be more profitable next year, or have you hit your peak? The goal should be to sell a business when it's at the top of its game—not before, not after.

Be sure to also think about how the sale will affect your relationship with the company. Some deals require entrepreneurs to stay on for a certain number of months or years once the sale is complete. This is primarily to help ensure a smooth transition for the new owners. While this may sound like an easy request, many entrepreneurs find it to be excruciating.

Not only will your role in the company change, but you'll have to watch someone else make crucial decisions that have a massive impact on your business. It's possible the new ownership will want to alter something you've spent years perfecting, or choose to go in a direction that you're completely against. Would you be required to change roles and stay at the company? Does the new owner expect you to act as a consultant or advisor for a certain period of time? Or would you be asked to leave immediately and sever all ties? Be sure to gauge expectations in advance, because they could potentially be deal breakers.

Selling a company can be thrilling. It is the final chapter of the story—the grand finale of the concerto. But be certain you're completely satisfied with the deal before signing on the dotted line. If a buyer is pressuring you to make a decision before you're ready, it's not the right buyer for you.

Think about every sleepless night you spent building the company. Recall that one huge sale you made or that major deal that landed at just the right time. Remember how it felt the first time you called yourself an entrepreneur—the first time you said it out loud. Your business took time and care to build, and you owe it to yourself and your organization to give the decision to sell the same sort of careful consideration.

While it can be both fulfilling and rewarding, letting your business go can also be a scary process—but don't let it get the best of you. The greatest thing about being a builder, a maker, a doer, is that there's always the next: the next project, the next business, the next chapter. Whatever decision you make, don't forget the most important thing: You are an entrepreneur. You'll make it work. You always do.

SHARK BITE

"Before you can even think about selling your company you need a stabilized business model. People buy businesses because they think they can enhance the revenue or profits, not because they want to take on an inordinate risk."

KEVIN

ARE YOU WORTH IT?
DETERMINING YOUR VALUATION

Hands down, the most tumultuous and impassioned conversations that happen in the Shark Tank are around a company's valuation—its economic value. Determining how much a business is worth is not an easy thing to do. While cash flow and profit are easy to measure, growth is not.

Businesses are evaluated differently depending on their specific industry. For example, according to the *Business Reference Guide* published by Business Brokerage Press, the "rule of thumb" valuation for a flower shop is 30 to 35 percent of annual sales plus inventory, while the valuation for a veterinary practice is 70 percent of annual revenues plus inventory. You can find plenty of charts online to cross-check your specific industry, some of which are listed in the Tools and Resources section of this book.

It's nearly impossible to accurately valuate a business that hasn't begun bringing in cash. But for those that have started making money, there are various methods for discovering the business's worth. Below are three ways to begin calculating yours:

Step One: Identify the revenue stream
Make sure you know how much pre-tax revenue you're bringing in annually. Depending on the industry and the buyer, your valuation might be a multiple of that revenue (e.g., three times annual revenue).

Step Two: Determine the cost of your assets
Besides just the revenue and profits of your business, a buyer will also be inheriting your assets (e.g., equipment, real estate, furniture). It's important to know how much your assets are worth, so you can include them in the price.

Step Three: Examine the profits

What are your company's earnings? In other words, how much money do you have after you've paid your expenses? This will play a key role in your overall valuation.

While each of these steps is significant, there are plenty of other factors that may help determine your valuation. For example, you could find a buyer who has strategic reasons for acquiring your company. Perhaps your local competition is interested in purchasing your business in order to gain a larger share of the market. That changes the game entirely.

You never want to leave money on the table when valuating your business, but you also must not price yourself out of the market. The more research you do, the more likely it is that you'll be able to negotiate the best deal possible.

LANI LAZZARI, SIMPLE SUGARS (SEASON 4)

BIG IDEA: All-natural skincare products designed especially for sensitive skin.
INVESTOR: Mark Cuban

For many entrepreneurs there is one defining moment, one serendipitous collision of scattered events that come together at just the right time and create that initial spark of ingenuity and innovation. For Lani Lazzari, that moment occurred shortly after her eleventh birthday.

Suffering with eczema since birth, Lani constantly struggled to find skin care products. Fed up with the search, the tween entrepreneur decided to make one herself. "I started researching ingredients and eventually created a product that, for the first time ever, completely took away my eczema," recounts Lani. "Nothing had ever worked before. It was amazing."

While the homemade scrubs proved effective, it's very possible they never would have made their way out of the house, if not for what occurred next.

A few months after inventing the product, Lani's mother, a successful pharmaceutical salesperson, was passed over for a promised promotion while on maternity leave. When she eventually returned to work, she was asked to leave.

"It was such a difficult experience for my mom," says Lani. "After watching her go through that, I was really discouraged about going into the corporate world one day, especially as a woman."

As the holidays approached, Lani's family decided to scale back by making homemade Christmas gifts—a perfect opportunity for the budding skin care enthusiast to share her hand-crafted scrubs. Almost instantly, the feedback came pouring in.

Everyone went crazy for the product, and it completely took away her aunt's psoriasis. As more people began requesting the scrubs, Lani realized she had a full-fledged business on her hands and decided to officially launch Simple Sugars.

At first, Lani sold her products at craft shows and home parties, but as orders began to pick up, she knew it was time to up the ante. At only seventeen, Lani worked with her school to arrange a year of independent study so she could focus on building the company. It was the first time she was able to devote all her energy to growing the business, and not surprisingly, things quickly began taking off.

But as Simple Sugars blossomed, Lani needed more capital. As a young person, it was difficult for her to secure a loan, so she turned to *Shark Tank* for an investment to help grow the company. After making a deal with Mark Cuban, Simple Sugars went from a small, humble business to an in-demand power-house.

"We ended up getting fifteen thousand orders in the three days after my episode aired," says Lani. "To put that in perspective, during the previous year we received a total of thirteen hundred orders. Just six weeks after our episode aired, we had received twenty-two thousand orders."

Like any rapid growth, however, it didn't come without its challenges. With such a large number of orders, Lani's company went from five to fifteen employees almost overnight, which of course required many hours of hiring and training. What's more, her fulfillment center was not prepared to handle the volume, and she was forced to immediately find a new vendor. "It was difficult," Lani explains. "But it was definitely worth it."

Today, at nineteen years old, Lani is proof that running a successful business isn't about age or experience, but about tireless motivation, endless hard work, and unquenchable passion. Although Lani has ambitious sales goals, she hasn't forgotten about one of her primary reasons for starting the business in the first place.

"After watching what my mom went through, I made the decision to create a company with a really great culture. You shouldn't have to choose between having a life you love and a job you love. I've always believed you can have both."

To find out more about Lani and Simple Sugars, visit SimpleSugars.MyShopify.com or follow them on Twitter @simplesugars

REAL-WORLD WISDOM: "You can't let fear get in the way. It's not going to be easy, and you're definitely going to make a lot of mistakes. But you can't let that stop you from ever trying. You'll figure things out as you go."

PART SIX

A DIP IN THE TANK: BEHIND THE SCENES AT *SHARK TANK*

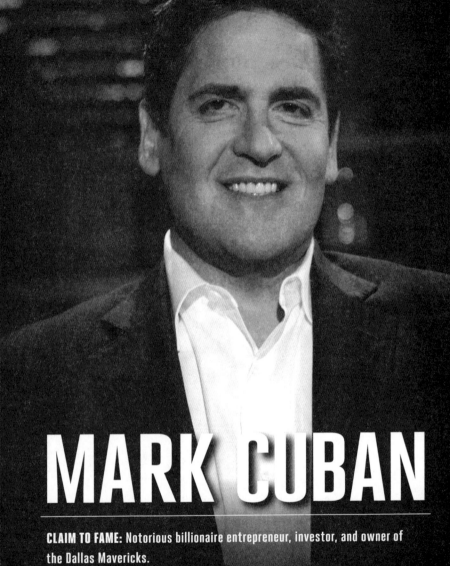

MARK CUBAN

CLAIM TO FAME: Notorious billionaire entrepreneur, investor, and owner of the Dallas Mavericks.

THE WAY I WORK: "The most important element to my success is that I out-worked everyone. I made sure that I knew more about my business and industry than anyone else. If you want to be successful, you have to be willing to work hard."

IT ONLY TAKES ONE

The reason I'm successful is because I outworked everyone else. I worked jobs I didn't like. I worked jobs I loved but that had no chance of becoming careers. I worked jobs that barely paid the rent. I had so many jobs my parents wondered if I would ever be stable.

With every effort, I learned more. With every mistake and failure, not just mine, but those around me, I learned what not to do. I had more than a healthy dose of fear, an unlimited amount of hope, and more importantly, no limit on time and effort.

I read every book or magazine I could get my hands on. Heck, it costs three bucks for a magazine, twenty bucks for a book. If it inspired one good idea that led to a customer or solution, it paid for itself.

No one really asks me about my adventures working for Mellon Bank, or Tronics 2000, or trying to start a business selling powdered milk (it was cheaper by the gallon, and I thought it tasted good). They don't ask me about working as a bartender or getting fired from my job at Your Business Software for wanting to close a sale rather than sweep the floors. No one ever asked me about what it was like when I started Micro Solutions and how I used to count the months I was in business, hoping to outlast my previous endeavors and make this one a success.

The point is that it doesn't matter how many times you strike out. No one is going to know or care about your failures, and neither should you. All you have to do is learn. Everything I read was public. Anyone could buy the same books and magazines. The same information was available to anyone who wanted it. Turns out most people didn't want it.

In business, to be a success, you only have to be right once—one single, solitary time—and you are set for life. That's the beauty of the business world. Just get it right once.

15

SWIMMING WITH THE SHARKS: A ROUNDTABLE Q&A

A business can't exist without an entrepreneur and *Shark Tank* couldn't exist without the Sharks. Together, Robert Herjavec, Lori Greiner, Barbara Corcoran, Kevin O'Leary, Daymond John, and Mark Cuban provide a wide range of talents and skills that have helped countless businesses achieve unimaginable results. From tech companies to bakeries, these six disciplined investors have demonstrated an extraordinary ability to evolve and grow companies of all shapes and sizes. But how and why were these six chosen?

"When we were putting the show together, we spent a lot of time making sure we found the right Sharks," says executive producer Clay Newbill. "We were looking at a lot of people. Not only did we want to find a group of extremely successful entrepreneurs and investors, we wanted to make sure they had diversified portfolios."

But diversity is about more than just a portfolio. Each Shark represents his or her own specific approach to business and investing. Robert's point of view may be quite different from

Lori's or Kevin's—and in fact it is. A quality that attracts one Shark to an entrepreneur may be the very thing that turns off another Shark completely. And while these varying perspectives can create tension, they ultimately help give *Shark Tank* its spark. Perhaps more important, this broad array of ideologies represents a larger truth that you're bound to experience when starting your own business: there is no template for success. The Sharks don't use a formula when evaluating a company; there's no special algorithm to guarantee a return. All they have to rely on is their own knowledge, experience, and gut instinct.

"Sharks are unpredictable," says Newbill. "If you're in the water and you see one coming towards you, you don't know what will happen. Will it swim past you? Will it take a bite? Maybe it will take a bite out of another Shark. The same thing is true on the show. You never know what's going to happen."

Each week on *Shark Tank* you learn a little more about each Shark, but there's more to these six passionate investors than what you see on-camera. It's their small, subtle idiosyncrasies that make them unique, and it's these same distinct characteristics that play an integral role in their investment decisions. Whether or not you ever get the chance to pitch your business to the Sharks, knowing more about who they are and what they value can only make for a more exciting viewing experience.

As the author of *Shark Tank Jump Start Your Business*, I've been given a very unique and special opportunity to get to know the Sharks outside of the tank. After spending time with each individually via phone calls, emails, and in-person meetings, we all gathered together during the taping of the fifth season for a roundtable discussion to dig deeper into their philosophies about business and investing, to answer some of the most highly requested viewer questions, and to uncover more valuable advice for present and future entrepreneurs.

THE CONVERSATION

The Sharks
BACK ROW (*left to right*): Daymond John, Barbara Corcoran, Robert Herjavec
FRONT ROW (*left to right*): Mark Cuban, Kevin O'Leary, Lori Greiner

MICHAEL PARRISH DUDELL: People choose to start businesses for a variety of reasons—one of the most common and perhaps elusive of which is to satisfy a passion. What role do you think passion should play in the life of a business and entrepreneur?

BARBARA CORCORAN: First, let me start by saying that passion can blind you, but it can also give you clarity of vision at the same time. And often it does both. It's dangerous to be blinded by the love of what you're doing, but you almost have to be that dumb to see your plan through to the end.

LORI GREINER: Barbara's right. I really believe that if you want to succeed you have to be passionate about what you're doing.

DAYMOND JOHN: Yeah, but what's most important is that you're passionate about the process of running a business. If somebody wants to be a designer and all they care about is their art or vision, you could call them passionate, but that's not necessarily the right kind of passion to have. If you *really* care about your art, you need to be passionate about the actual running of the business.

MARK CUBAN: I think passion is overrated. Everyone has a lot of passions. I have a passion for sports—a passion for music. That doesn't make it a business, and that doesn't make you qualified to run the business. So you should never start a business based on a passion. It's really about where you put your efforts. If you're willing to work hard at something and put effort into it, a passion will naturally develop. Effort should come first. You should see what you're good at and go from there.

ROBERT HERJAVEC: Yeah, but you've got to love it, Mark. You're going to be working on your business 24/7, and if you don't love what you're doing you won't last. I'm sitting here right now on my email; I'll be flying all night after we're done taping; I'll be on email for another nine hours once I leave here. And yeah, I'm complaining about it, but I love it. If you don't wake up excited to go to work every day, how can you survive?

LORI GREINER: We all love what we do, right? Most entrepreneurs are driven by passion and that's why we don't mind doing it 24/7.

KEVIN O'LEARY: But I think some entrepreneurs use "passion" as an excuse to avoid focusing on performance metrics. In other words, they think being passionate about something should give them a free pass to fail.

ROBERT HERJAVEC: Right. I think some entrepreneurs use it as an excuse when their business isn't making money. But if a business isn't making money, it's not a business. It's a hobby.

KEVIN O'LEARY: So for me it's just a default. I expect people to be passionate about their work, but I don't care about it. What I care about is if it helps them drive metrics of performance. In the case of a startup, are they achieving sales? In the case of a more mature business, are they maintaining or growing margins? And if they can't do that, I'd rather fire them and find a better executor. In the end, businesses that succeed and make money for shareholders are built around execution.

MICHAEL PARRISH DUDELL: So I think it's clear you all feel very differently about the topic, which actually speaks to a much larger issue. While each of you has achieved success, you represent a variety of different ideologies. In fact, the only thing you really do have in common is that you've put in tremendous time and effort into building your businesses. You've all put in the work. Today, there's so much talk about optimizing a business and working smarter instead of working harder. When it comes to real, sustainable success, do you think there's something to be said for good old-fashioned sweat equity?

KEVIN O'LEARY: It's a given that you have to put in the work. But as an investor I don't care how much time it's taken for an entrepreneur to build a business. All I care about is if the business is making money.

LORI GREINER: But sometimes seeing that a person has worked hard and persisted shows you something about their character. It shows you they have the stamina and perseverance to not just give up when things get hard. And to me that's an important trait for a partner to have. I want to know that my partner has the drive and tenacity it takes to put in the time and hard work.

DAYMOND JOHN: Look, you'll never be able to optimize your business 100 percent. Until you exit the company, there's always going to be more to do, more hours to put in. If you don't want to work the hours, you shouldn't be an entrepreneur.

MARK CUBAN: Right. Putting in the hours has always mattered, and it always will.

DAYMOND JOHN: If one part of the business is doing well, most good entrepreneurs will switch focus and try to expand another part of the business. The goal shouldn't be to work less.

MICHAEL PARRISH DUDELL: Let's talk about failure for a second. Individually, each of you has spoken with me about the value of failure—that sometimes failure in the short term can lead to success in the long term. Are there any specific lessons that you've learned through failure that may be helpful to new entrepreneurs?

ROBERT HERJAVEC: I hate to use the word "failure." I prefer to say challenges or stumbling blocks. The only time you really fail is when you give up. There's been a lot of crap that's happened to me in business, just like everyone at this table, but I don't think entrepreneurs view that kind of stuff as failure. Failure feels so finite.

LORI GREINER: One of my favorite quotes is "Failure is not an option; it's a state of mind." And that's true. I don't think any of us look at "failure" as failure. I think we look at it as a new challenge to overcome.

BARBARA CORCORAN: Here's a great example. In Season 3 I invested in a company called Daisy Cakes. The founder was doing so well so quickly that we took her to three large bakeries and reconfigured all of her recipes so she could produce on a mass scale. Well guess what? It didn't work. The reconfiguration was wrong, and two of the three bakeries were unreliable. And you know what? She lost a ton of money, and guess where she is now? She's making cakes back in her little kitchen. But all of the quality control issues are gone, and her business is doing really well. She's smarter now and more prepared for what's ahead. She had to take a step back before she could move forward. She's a walking, talking example of someone who has handled failure the right way.

MICHAEL PARRISH DUDELL: Each of you seems to have certain types of companies that you prefer to invest in. Is that true? Are there certain industries that you favor and others that you try to avoid? For instance, Daymond, I know you don't usually invest in food-related businesses.

BARBARA CORCORAN: Yeah. Why is that, Daymond?

DAYMOND JOHN: Because I was the one at Red Lobster taking boxes of frozen shrimp home every day and selling it to the Chinese place around the corner. Businesses that involve food or perishable items typically have smaller margins and are less reliable. If Hurricane Sandy hits, for instance, and you have a bunch of product in a warehouse in New Jersey, you're immediately out $10 million worth of goods.

BARBARA CORCORAN: See, and I love food businesses because it's not complicated. You see what you're selling, who's going to buy it, and you ship it. That's not so bad. It's not so sophisticated.

DAYMOND JOHN: Yeah, but look at what happened with the Daisy Cakes thing. I'm never going to have the wrong formula on a T-shirt.

BARBARA CORCORAN: That's a good point. I think that was a case of too much growth too soon.

MARK CUBAN: I like to invest in tech companies. I try to stick to what I know.

LORI GREINER: Personally I like anything that I think is going to be great on the market. It can be in any industry as long as I think it's going to really sell. I just like great products and great businesses. I need to be excited by it.

ROBERT HERJAVEC: I don't look at a specific industry; I prefer to work with an entrepreneur who knows a market. You have to know your industry inside and out because that's something

I can't bring to the table. So it's not a matter of industry for me; it's the entrepreneur.

KEVIN O'LEARY: And I could care less about that. I'm more concerned about the product and market than I am about the entrepreneur. People are interchangeable. If someone can't perform, I'll take them out behind the barn and shoot them. I have no problem doing that. And it's important that the entrepreneurs I work with understand that about me. I think this whole idea that you care about the person and that they matter is stupid. I couldn't care at all. I just want to make money.

LORI GREINER: That's amazing. It's so the complete opposite for me.

KEVIN O'LEARY: And look, we both have success so we're both right. I mean personally I think I'm more right.

BARBARA CORCORAN: Oh Kevin, I don't believe any of that crap you're always saying.

LORI GREINER: I know. I can't believe this is real. I just feel like humanity is so important. It isn't always just about money. These are people we're talking about.

KEVIN O'LEARY: Oh, come on! Business is about money. That's it. Look, after I invested in Wicked Good Cupcakes, the daughter actually cried. She told her mother that I was the worst devil in the world.

BARBARA CORCORAN: She was right.

KEVIN O'LEARY: But Barbara, we've made so much money together now she calls me "Daddy." It's ridiculous. That business is up 10,000 percent.

LORI GREINER: But don't you ever care about anybody? Don't you ever feel something about the people, their families, their life, their passion, anything? Are you always so cold?

KEVIN O'LEARY: We're talking business here, aren't we? I think you have to separate personal from business. If you get emotionally involved with someone in business, it clouds your decision-making ability. That's a huge mistake. Because the reality is that as investors we're not right all the time. And sometimes you have to make tough decisions in the moment because you don't always know beforehand which businesses are going to fail and which are going to be a huge hit.

LORI GREINER: I don't think it's that much of a crapshoot though. If you have experience and intelligence, you know pretty quickly which businesses are going to work and which aren't. I always go with my gut and my experience. I can usually tell if it's going to be a winner or not.

BARBARA CORCORAN: I don't think it's that easy to tell. You can make an educated guess. That's about all.

MICHAEL PARRISH DUDELL: This may seem a little off topic, but I want to discuss the parallels between art and business. Kevin you're a photographer. Lori you used to be a playwright. Mark, you love film and music. Do you think there's a parallel between artistry and entrepreneurship?

MARK CUBAN: I think it's about logic and the way people think. If you're a musician, you know how to combine notes in the right way to make a song. That same process can easily be applied to building a business. It's like programming. Musicians are better programmers. Programmers understand logic. Logic is required to run a business.

KEVIN O'LEARY: I think there's a great balance in the karma of business: the yin and yang. Art is about chaos; business is about discipline. A person needs both.

MARK CUBAN: Kevin, if there's karma in business, you would be dead.

KEVIN O'LEARY: It's great to have both because they balance each other out. After a tough day of doing deals, there's nothing like rocking out with your band. I do that every Thursday night at 9 P.M.

ROBERT HERJAVEC: He's a great guitar player.

BARBARA CORCORAN: I can't picture it. I just can't.

KEVIN O'LEARY: Our band is smoking hot.

BARBARA CORCORAN: I'm sure it is. But do you wear a wig? I just can't picture it.

LORI GREINER: What kind of stuff do you play?

KEVIN O'LEARY: Lately we've been trying to get into the whole Steely Dan portfolio.

DAYMOND JOHN: Wait, you actually have a band? Who the hell wants to see you play?

KEVIN O'LEARY: We just practice. We rent out a space and just rock out for the hell of it. We don't play in front of crowds.

ROBERT HERJAVEC: I think when you run this hard you've got to have something like that. Mark owns a basketball team. I race cars. Kevin plays guitar.

KEVIN O'LEARY: I don't think you race cars, Robert. You crash cars.

ROBERT HERJAVEC: That's probably true.

LORI GREINER: It's all about creativity. An entrepreneur needs to be creative, so naturally they're attracted to creative activities outside of work.

MICHAEL PARRISH DUDELL: Let's move on to education. I think the conversation around education has changed dramatically in the last ten or fifteen years, especially when it comes to higher education. Do you think an entrepreneur should get an MBA? Yes or no?

KEVIN O'LEARY: Absolutely not. Completely irrelevant.

DAYMOND JOHN: You don't need it.

LORI GREINER: Irrelevant.

ROBERT HERJAVEC: Waste of time.

MARK CUBAN: Waste of time and money.

BARBARA CORCORAN: I'll tell you what, it gets most entrepreneurs into trouble. They think too fancy. They complicate things. All of a sudden they think they have the magic formula. Having an MBA and being good at business aren't related at all.

LORI GREINER: Yeah, it doesn't mean anything. Some of the most successful people in the world didn't even graduate from high school.

KEVIN O'LEARY: I agree with Barbara and Lori. An education is no prerequisite for success at any level whether that's high school, college, or an MBA.

DAYMOND JOHN: Wait now. I don't want to give a message to kids that they shouldn't go to school. Getting an education is important.

KEVIN O'LEARY: We didn't say it wasn't.

MARK CUBAN: But you don't need an MBA. Do the math. You'd be an idiot to get an MBA with how much those things cost today.

DAYMOND JOHN: But an entrepreneur still needs to understand the basics—things like accounting. You still need to learn that kind of stuff. That's all I'm saying.

MICHAEL PARRISH DUDELL: Even though each of you is an entrepreneur at the core, on *Shark Tank* you're acting as an investor, which requires you to wear a very different hat. How did you make the leap from entrepreneur to investor?

KEVIN O'LEARY: I decided I didn't want to be the sole executioner anymore. I wanted a diversified portfolio with a variety of high-performing companies. That's how you achieve real success.

LORI GREINER: I've just always been doing it all along. As I've grown my business I've invested in others too.

DAYMOND JOHN: For me, it goes back to your first question about passion. Do you love the business or do you love the product or service? Designers often think that success will never end. But of course that's not true. This too shall pass. That's my motto. Whether it's good times or bad times, you have to remember that this too shall pass. When I first started, I looked out in the market and saw all these other fashion lines that swore they'd be around forever and were gone within a few years. So I started investing in other companies because I recognized that no matter how well my business did, it was eventually going to end. That's how I made the decision to invest.

BARBARA CORCORAN: I took the leap from investor rather blindly, and frankly I probably have no business being here. That's the truth. I knew real estate. I knew sales. When I started investing, I took on some really terrible businesses.

DAYMOND JOHN: But that's not true. You're not new to investing You've invested in real estate for a long time.

BARBARA CORCORAN: Yeah, but that's my game.

DAYMOND JOHN: But you've been an investor for a while. You just altered what type of investments you can make.

BARBARA CORCORAN: That's right.

MICHAEL PARRISH DUDELL: Personally, I think the best investors bring more than just cash to the table. Besides capital, what do you feel is your greatest contribution as an investor?

KEVIN O'LEARY: First, I think we bring the celebrity of *Shark Tank* that's attached to us now. Number two we bring contacts. Every one of us has a huge Rolodex, and we generally get our calls returned. We all have experience in different sectors, so a lot depends on what the entrepreneur is selling. But I think at the end of the day success boils down to the market, the product, and the person. We just add a little extra sauce.

DAYMOND JOHN: Also, I think what we all bring is our knowledge and experience. We make sure they don't pull the trigger too soon or make a move they'll regret later. Really, I think our knowledge is our greatest asset.

MARK CUBAN: It's like anything, right? *Shark Tank* can provide that extra jump start for a business, but it's up to the entrepreneur after that.

TEN THINGS TO KNOW BEFORE ENTERING THE SHARK TANK

There's no doubt about it: walking into the Tank can be a stressful experience. But it doesn't have to be. Having a great product or service is important, but the best way to ensure success is to be as prepared, poised, and professional as possible. Here are ten tips from *Shark Tank* executive producers Mark Burnett and Clay Newbill that every entrepreneur should know before going head-to-head with the Sharks—or any potential investors.

1. Be able to communicate your business masterfully: Before speaking with investors it's crucial that you're able to articulate certain key areas of your business. What's your business model? What problem are you trying to solve? Who does your company serve? Not only should you be able to painlessly answers these types of questions, you must do so in a way that's clear and concise.

2. Know your numbers: It can't be stressed enough: if you want to succeed in the tank, you *must* know your numbers backwards and forwards. From revenues and expenses to projections and manufacturing costs, be ready to answer any and all financial queries. Remember, the Sharks are powerhouse investors; they expect your numbers to add up.

3. Research each Shark thoroughly: You know more about the Sharks than they know about you. Use that to your advantage. Do you homework and uncover everything you can about each of their personal and professional histories. The more information you have, the more targeted your pitch can be.

4. Prepare for all potential questions: You don't necessarily need to study every single episode of *Shark Tank* like Cousins Maine Lobster founders Jim Tselikis and Sabin Lomac did, but it's important to be prepared for any question the Sharks might ask. Does one particular area of your business make you uncomfortable? Don't run from it. That's probably the area that needs the most preparation.

5. Be honest and forthright: The very worst thing you can do in the tank is be dishonest or conniving. If you don't have an answer to a particular question, it's better to be truthful and look unprepared than it is to make something up. Don't forget, there's a lengthy due diligence process once the deal is made.

6. Articulate your growth strategy: The Sharks only want to invest in companies they believe have real growth potential. By articulating your strategy during the pitch, you will help them understand how you plan to grow your business. They want to know that you have a plan to take the company to the next level.

7. Address your weaknesses: Every business has an Achilles' heel. That's a definite. So there's no reason to avoid it or run from it. Don't just be aware of your weaknesses, but embrace them and be able to address them in a straightforward way. Make no mistake about it: if there's a glaring hole in your business, the Sharks will find it.

8. Play up your secret sauce: What's your niche? What's your most valuable and compelling differentiator? Whatever it may be, make sure it's included in your pitch. Chances are you have many competitors. The Sharks anticipate that. What you must prove is that there's something special that sets your business apart.

9. Exude confidence: Everyone's attracted to confidence, especially the Sharks. From the moment you walk into the room, be cognizant of how you're presenting yourself. What's your body language like? Is your voice strong and confident or weak and shallow? You may be surprised at just how much charisma and confidence can help you succeed. Remember, you were chosen to be on *Shark Tank* for a reason. Act like it.

10. Show appreciation and graciousness: Maybe you'll get a deal. Maybe you won't. No matter what happens in the tank, don't forget to always be appreciative and gracious. As

SoundBender founder Rabbi Moshe Weiss pointed out, this is an opportunity to appeal not just to the Sharks but to your customers and the larger business community as well. Dignity and manners count for a lot.

To find out more about how you can appear on *Shark Tank*, visit ABC.com/SharkTank.

TRACEY NOONAN AND DANIELLE DESROCHES, WICKED GOOD CUPCAKES (SEASON 4)

BIG IDEA: Gourmet cupcakes for all occasions that can be shipped in a jar nationwide.

INVESTOR: Kevin O'Leary

For Tracey Noonan, watching her youngest daughter Danielle leave home was difficult. Tracey had always been close to her children, and the thought of an empty nest left the mother of three feeling unsettled. Determined to maintain a close relationship, Tracey and Danielle decided to take a cake decorating class together once a week at a local bakery. Never did they imagine this seemingly insignificant hobby would turn into a full-fledged business.

Shortly after the first class, the duo discovered that they had a natural talent for baking. "People would literally stand in front of us and moan as they ate our cupcakes," says Tracey. "They just loved everything about them."

Working out of their home kitchen, Tracey and Danielle began getting more time-consuming orders and eventually even secured a handful of corporate clients. After two exceptionally large orders and some unplanned press, the mother-and-daughter team knew it was time to turn their hobby into a business.

"Neither my daughter nor I graduated from college," says Tracey. "And I guess in some small way I felt like we had something to prove. We knew we had a great idea and people loved the product, so we decided to take the leap."

Shortly after their decision to move forward, Tracey and her husband invested money from their 401K to open the first Wicked Good Cupcakes shop in South Shore, Massachusetts, just outside the city of Boston. A big fan of *Shark Tank*, Tracey decided to fill out an online application shortly after opening the store, and eventually she made it onto the show. Less than a year after their official launch, Tracey and Danielle were partners with Kevin O'Leary.

Given only two weeks to prepare before their episode aired, Tracey and Danielle began scrambling to get everything in place. Thanks to a lot of tireless work, and the fact that Tracey's husband is a technologist by trade, their website withstood the heavy traffic and Wicked Good Cupcakes was able to capitalize on all the attention. In the week following the episode, the bakery did $230,000 in gross sales—almost as much as they had sold in the entire previous year.

Today, Wicked Good Cupcakes has a second location, in Faneuil Hall—the fourth largest tourist attraction in America—and is continuing to grow and expand. Exactly how big can a cupcake empire get? You'll have to keep your eye on Tracey and Danielle to find out!

To find out more, visit WickedGoodCupcakes.com or follow them on Twitter @wkdgoodcupcakes.

REAL-WORLD WISDOM: "Never let anyone say no. You can't let that be an option. When we started this business, many people told us that it was a dumb idea and that we shouldn't do it. But we refused to let that get in our way. If you want to succeed, you can never take no for an answer!"

FINAL WORDS

*S*hark Tank Jump Start Your Business isn't just a catchy title; it's a call to action—a declaration of opportunity. While the primary goal of this book has been to provide the knowledge and insights you need to successfully launch a business, its greater purpose is much more profound than that.

Starting a business is a marathon, not a sprint. And whether you find yourself standing at mile one or mile twenty-five, rest assured the race has only just begun. By offering a mix of useful information, words of wisdom from entrepreneurs who have appeared on the show, and advice from the Sharks themselves, this book is more than just a guidebook. It's a tool to connect the dots between what you see on *Shark Tank* and what you experience in your own life.

It may not be clear from your vantage point, but you already have a great deal in common with the Sharks and entrepreneurs who enter the Tank. Just like you, each one of them made the decision to believe, to tinker, to take action. Just like you, they overcame barriers large and small. And although today they are defined by their successes, they were undoubtedly shaped by their failures—just like you will be.

The path you've chosen is full of many highs and lows. But of course you already knew that. And while it's rare you'll uncover "right" answers or "perfect" choices, there is one constant you can rely on: your own ability to persist and persevere. The greatest lesson you can take away from this book is that with hard work, discipline, and focus come tremendous rewards. It's you who's in control of your future—no one else.

Good luck on your journey, and thank you for being a part of this one.

TOOLS AND RESOURCES

MY SMALL BUSINESS JUMP START

MY BIG IDEA:
MY TARGET MARKET:

Demographic:
Geographic location:
Wants and needs:
Hobbies and activities:
Overall market size:

MY COMPETITION:

Competitor 1:
How I'm different:

Competitor 2:
How I'm different:

Competitor 3:
How I'm different:

MY NAME:

_____ Check patent
_____ Check online search
_____ Open social media accounts in that name

MY MISSION STATEMENT:

_____
_____
_____
_____

MY TWO-MINUTE PITCH :

_____
_____
_____
_____

FROM IDEA TO INCORPORATION: A FLOWCHART

Incorporating your business is an important part of getting your venture up and running. But for the first-time entrepreneur, it can often feel complicated and unnerving. Below you'll find a flowchart designed to help add some additional clarity to the process. Keep in mind that while this chart is a quick way to identify which incorporation structure is best for your business, you may still wish to seek out the assistance of an accountant or lawyer. Depending on the type of company you're starting, there may be some important details to consider. For instance, certain types of companies, like banks and insurance agencies, must follow very specific guidelines.

YOUR IDEA

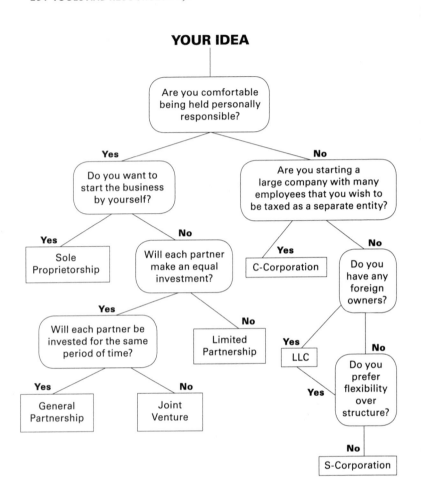

TALK THE TALK: SMALL BUSINESS TERMS TO KNOW

Accrual method: An accounting method wherein revenue is recorded when the order occurs or the service is provided and not when the payment is received, and expenses are accounted for when they are incurred and not when they are paid.

Affiliate marketing: A type of performance-based marketing where affiliates are compensated for each visitor or customer delivered.

Angel investor: An individual who provides capital for a business in exchange for debt or equity ownership.

Assets: Anything of economic value that a company owns, including property and equipment.

Banner ad: A graphic or image used on a website to advertise a product or service.

Barriers to entry: Obstacles that prevent competitors from easily entering an industry or business.

Business model: The method by which an organization generates revenue and makes a profit.

Business plan: A set of documents that outlines the goals of a business and the steps required to achieve them.

Capital: Money invested in a business with the purpose of generating income.

Cash flow: Incomings and outgoings of cash that represent the operating activities of a business.

Cash Method: An accounting method wherein revenue is recorded when the payment is actually received, and expenses are accounted for when they are actually paid.

Consumer segment: A group of consumers who possess specific similarities, such as gender, location, or spending habits.

Convertible debt: A bond that can be converted into a predetermined amount of equity ownership.

Due diligence: The process of researching and validating specific material facts related to a potential investment or sale.

Equity ownership: An ownership interest in an organization expressed in the form of stock.

Fixed cost: Regular operating costs a business accrues on a weekly, monthly, or yearly basis not associated with the individual cost (variable cost) of producing the actual product or service. EXAMPLE: Rent and equipment.

Franchise: A business system wherein a party (the franchisor) allows another party (the franchisee) the right to produce and/or sell a product or service.

Franchisee: An individual who purchases a franchise business.

Franchisor: A company that allows an individual to open and run a location of their business.

Fringe benefits: Nontaxable benefits provided by an employer that supplement an employee's salary.

Gross profit: A company's total amount of revenue minus the cost to produce the product without deductions (or the variable costs). EXAMPLE: It costs $10 to make a product and you sell it for $25. Your gross profit is $15.

Hard launch: A method of launching a new business to the general public.

Independent contractor: A self-employed individual who provides specific services to a business or on behalf of one.

Intellectual property: Knowledge, creative ideas, or expressions of the human mind that have commercial value and are protectable under law.

Letter of intent: A nonbinding document that expresses the interest of an individual or business in purchasing another business.

Liabilities: Anything of economic value that a company owes to others, including debts and obligations.

Marketing: The activities of an organization related to buying or selling a product or service.

Market share: A percentage of total sales volume in a market captured by a brand, product, or organization.

Markup: An amount added to the cost of a product or service by the seller to cover expenses and profit.

Metrics: The measurement used to determine a quantifiable element of a company's performance.

Mission statement: A written assertion of an organization's core purpose and intention.

Net profit: A company's gross profit minus any deductions. EXAMPLE: The same company that sells a $10 product for $25 must also factor in their office space, equipment, and other fixed costs. Once that's subtracted from their $15 gross profit they will have their net profit.

Net worth: The monetary value of a company, figured by subtracting the total dollar amount of liabilities from the total dollar amount of assets. Also known as net value or equity.

Profit margin: A ratio of profit, often expressed as a percentage, earned from the sale of a product or service.

Proof of concept: Evidence that establishes that an idea, invention, process, or business model is feasible.

Public relations: The practice of promoting and maintaining the positive image of an organization through outside media and other nonpaid forms of communication.

Revenue: Income generated from the sale of a product or service before costs or expenses are deducted.

Soft launch: A method of launching a business to a limited audience, often used to test the viability of a product or service.

Supply chain: A network of different organizations or individuals that play a role in the production or delivery of a product or service to a consumer.

Target market: A specific market segment at which a company aims its products or services.

Turnkey operation: A business that can be started with no additional work from a buyer.

Value proposition: A business statement that clearly explains why a consumer should buy a product or service.

Variable costs: Costs that change frequently based on a company's level of activity or a specific business variable. EXAMPLE: production, labor, and material.

Vendor: Any outside company or individual that provides goods or services to an organization

Venture capitalist: A private investor or group of investors who provide(s) a very large sum of capital to promising ventures in exchange for equity ownership.

ONLINE RESOURCES

PART ONE
TO BE OR NOT TO BE . . . AN ENTREPRENEUR

General Small Business Publications
Entrepreneur: http://www.Entrepreneur.com
Fast Company: http://www.FastCompany.com
Forbes: http://www.Forbes.com
Fortune: http://www.Fortune.com
Harvard Business Review: http://www.HBR.org
INC.: http://www.INC.com

Education
General Assembly: https://generalassemb.ly
Marie Forleo's B-School: http://rhhbschool.com
MBA Programs: http://www.mbaprograms.org
Personal MBA: http://www.PersonalMBA.com
TED: http://www.Ted.com

Community
CoFoundr: http://cofoundr.com
Entrepreneur Connect: http://econnect.entrepreneur.com
MeetUp: http://www.MeetUp.com
SBA Events: http://www.sba.gov/community/discuss-popular-topics
    /small-business-events

SCORE: http://www.score.org
StartUp Nation: http://www.startupnation.com
World Domination Summit: http://www.worlddominationsummit.com
Young Entrepreneur Council: http://www.TheYEC.org

Product Development/Inventor Tools
Industrial Design Society of America: http://www.idsa.org
Invention City: http://www.inventioncity.com
Inventor Resources US Government: http://www.uspto.gov/inventors
Quirky: http://quirky.com

Purchase a business/franchise
BizBuySell: http://www.bizbuysell.com
BizQuest: http://www.bizquest.com
Franchise: httpp://www.franchise.com
Franchise Opportunities: http://www.franchiseopportunities.com

PART TWO
SETTING UP SHOP

Market Research
American Time Use Survey: http://www.bls.gov/tus/home.htm
Census FactFinder: http://factfinder.census.gov
DemographicsNow: http://www.demographicsnow.com
MarketResearch: http://www.marketresearch.com

Business Plan
BPlans: http://www.bplans.com/sample_business_plans.php
Business Model Generation: http://www.businessmodelgeneration.com
    /canvas
Growth Wheel: http://www.growthwheel.com
INC.: http://www.inc.com/tools/business-plan-example.html
SBA: http://www.sba.gov/category/navigation-structure/starting
    -managing-business/starting-business/how-write-business-plan

Incorporation
Entrepreneur Magazine: http://www.entrepreneur.com/article/77730
ExpertLaw: http://www.expertlaw.com/library/business/incorporate_your
    self.html

Nolo: http://www.nolo.com/legal-encyclopedia/form-corporation-how
    -to-incorporate-30030.html
SBA: http://www.sba.gov/content/corporation
USA: http://www.usa.gov/Business/Incorporate.shtml

Insurance
Forbes: http://www.forbes.com/sites/thesba/2012/01/19/13-types-of
    -insurance-a-small-business-owner-should-have
Insure U for Small Business: http://www.insureuonline.org/smallbusiness
Legal Zoom: http://www.legalzoom.com/business-management/running
    -your-business/insuring-your-business-5-questions

Protecting Your Business
Google: http://www.google.com/?tbm_I>=pts
How Stuff Works: http://www.howstuffworks.com/patent1.htm
USPTO: http://www.uspto.gov/inventors/patents.jsp

PART THREE
MONEY MATTERS

Accounting
About.com: http://sbinformation.about.com/od/taxaccounting/Small
    _Business_Tax_Accounting.htm
Small Biz U: http://www.smallbizu.org/a101
Small Business Doer: http://www.smallbusinessdoer.com/online-accounting
    -software-review-and-comparison

Taxes
IRS: http://www.irs.gov/Businesses/Small-Businesses-&-Self-Employed
SBA: http://www.sba.gov/category/navigation-structure/starting-managing
    -business/starting-business/establishing-business/taxes
USA Today: http://www.usatoday.com/story/money/personalfinance
    /2013/03/14/taxes-entrepreneur-irs-small-business-tiips/1987289

Financing a Startup
Angel List: https://angel.co
HBS Elevator Pitch Builder: http://www.alumni.hbs.edu/careers/pitch
INC.: http://www.inc.com/guides/finance/20797.html
IndieGoGo: http://www.indiegogo.com
Kickstarter: http://www.kickstarter.com

Mashable: http://mashable.com/2011/04/12/tech-financing-changes
SBA: http://www.sba.gov/category/navigation-structure/loans-grants/small
-business-loans

PART FOUR
OPEN FOR BUSINESS

Vendors
Entrepreneur Magazine: http://www.entrepreneur.com/article/66028
Startup Nation: http://www.startupnation.com/business-articles/1293/1
/finding-manufacturer.asp

Finding Space
LifeHacker: http://lifehacker.com/5815881/how-can-i-work-from-home
-without-losing-touch
Loopnet: http://www.loopnet.com
Harvard Business Review: http://blogs.hbr.org/cs/2012/09/the_rise_of_co
-working_office.html
We Work: http://www.wework.com

Soft Launch vs. Hard
37 Signals: http://37signals.com/svn/posts/1759-why-its-wise-to-launch
-softly
CRN: http://www.crn.com/news/channel-programs/18827326/hard
-work-on-a-soft-launch-makes-a-lasting-impression.htm
LifeHack: http://www.lifehack.org/articles/featured/how-to-launch-a
-business-without-spending-a-dime.html

Productivity
99U: http://99u.com/articles/6585/10-laws-of-productivity
Forbes: http://www.forbes.com/sites/theyec/2012/11/26/7-web-productivity
-tools-thatll-maximize-your-efficiency/
PC Mag: http://www.pcmag.com/article2/0,2817,2395938,00.asp
Psychology Today: http://www.psychologytoday.com/basics/productivity

Marketing
Copyblogger: http://www.copyblogger.com/content-marketing
Duct Tape Marketing: http://www.ducttapemarketing.com/blog/category
/small-business-marketing

Fast Company: http://www.fastcompany.com/3007554/10-tips-small
-business-marketing-infusioncon

Hub Spot: http://www.hubspot.com/small-business-marketing-hub

Branding

Duct Tape Marketing: http://www.ducttapemarketing.com/blog/2012/12
/13/successful-small-business-brand

SlideShare: http://www.slideshare.net/coolstuff/the-brand-gap

Sales

Business Insider: http://www.businessinsider.com/learn-what-customer
-focus-really-means-in-sales-2011-1

Forbes: http://www.forbes.com/sites/mikemyatt/2012/05/01/to-increase
-revenue-stop-selling

INC.: http://www.inc.com/guides/2010/05/closing-the-sale.html

Startup Nation: http://www.startupnation.com/steps/71/3810/10/1/improve
-sales-techniques.htm

PART FIVE
TAKING IT TO THE NEXT LEVEL

Hiring

Freelancer: http://www.Freelancer.com

Guru.com: http://www.Guru.com

Monster: http://hiring.monster.com/hr/hr-best-practices/recruiting-hiring
-advice/strategic-workforce-planning/small-business-hiring-guide
.aspx

Wall Street Journal: http://guides.wsj.com/small-business/hiring-and
-managing-employees/how-to-hire-your-first-employee

Culture

Business Insider: http://www.businessinsider.com/tony-hsieh-creating-an
-amazing-company-culture-2013-3

Fast Company: http://www.fastcompany.com/1837853/8-rules-creating
-passionate-work-culture

Harvard Business Review: http://blogs.hbr.org/schwartz/2010/08/six
-secrets-to-creating-a-cult.html

New York Times: http://boss.blogs.nytimes.com/2013/05/21/the-real
-meaning-of-corporate-culture

Leadership

Psychology Today: http://www.psychologytoday.com/basics/leadership
LinkedIn: http://www.linkedin.com/today/post/article/20130128162711
-15077789-11-simple-concepts-to-become-a-better-leader
Technorati: http://technorati.com/business/gurus/article/5-reasons-why
-servant-leadership-works
Virgin: http://www.virgin.com/entrepreneur/blog/6-truths-of
-extraordinary-leadership

Growth

Evan Carmichael: http://www.evancarmichael.com/Business-Coach/154
/12-Step-Business-Growth-Plan.html
Fast Company: http://www.fastcompany.com/3004395/5-essential
-principles-growing-your-small-business
SBA: http://www.sba.gov/content/ideas-growing-your-business
Startup Nation: http://www.startupnation.com/business-articles/998/1
/AT_Business-Growth-Plan.asp

Franchising

Market Watch: http://www.marketwatch.com/story/thinking-about-a
-franchise-key-mistakes-to-avoid-2013-04-19
OpenForum: https://www.openforum.com/articles/top-4-mistakes-when
-franchising-your-business-a-small-business-guide
Small Biz Trends: http://smallbiztrends.com/2011/01/want-to-franchise
-a-business-5-sacred-rules-to-become-the-next-great-franchise.html

Selling Your Business

Business Week: http://www.businessweek.com/stories/2008-01-16/how
-to-sell-your-businessbusinessweek-business-news-stock-market-and
-financial-advice
INC.: http://www.inc.com/selling-a-business
Nolo: http://www.nolo.com/legal-encyclopedia/selling-business-eight
-steps-30143.html
New York Times: http://www.nytimes.com/2010/01/07/business
/smallbusiness/07guide.html?pagewanted_I>=all&_r_I>=0

BOOKS TO READ

More from the Sharks

The Brand Within: The Power of Branding from Birth to the Boardroom by Daymond John

Cold Hard Truth: On Business, Money & Life by Kevin O'Leary

Display of Power: How FUBU Changed a World of Fashion, Branding and Lifestyle by Daymond John

Driven: How to Succeed in Business and in Life by Robert Herjavec

How to Win at the Sport of Business: If I Can Do It, You Can Do It by Mark Cuban

Use What You've Got, and Other Business Lessons I Learned from My Mom by Barbara Corcoran and Bruce Littlefield

If You Don't Have Big Breasts, Put Ribbons on your Pigtails by Barbara Corcoran and Bruce Littlefield

Shark Tales: How I Turned $1,000 into a Billion Dollar Business by Barbara Corcoran

The Will to Win: Leading, Competing, Succeeding by Robert Herjavec

Must-Read Business Books

The 4-Hour Workweek: Escape 9–5, Live Anywhere, and Join the New Rich by Timothy Ferriss

The 22 Immutable Laws of Marketing: Violate Them at Your Own Risk! by Al Ries and Jack Trout

The $100 Startup: Reinvent the Way You Make a Living, Do What You Love, and Create a New Future by Chris Guillebeau

The Art of the Start: The Time-Tested, Battle-Hardened Guide for Anyone Starting Anything by Guy Kawasaki

The Brand Gap: How to Bridge the Distance Between Business Strategy and Design by Marty Neumeier

Crush It!: Why NOW Is the Time to Cash In on Your Passion by Gary Vaynerchuk

The E-Myth Revisited: Why Most Small Businesses Don't Work and What to Do About It by Michael E. Gerber

EntreLeadership: 20 Years of Practical Business Wisdom from the Trenches by Dave Ramsey

The Entrepreneur Equation: Evaluating the Realities, Risks, and Rewards of Having Your Own Business by Carol Roth and Michael Port

Good to Great: Why Some Companies Make the Leap . . . and Others Don't by Jim Collins

How to Win Friends & Influence People by Dale Carnegie

Influence: The Psychology of Persuasion by Robert B. Cialdini

I Will Teach You to Be Rich by Ramit Sethi

The Knack: How Street-Smart Entrepreneurs Learn to Handle Whatever Comes Up by Norm Brodsky and Bo Burlingham

The Lean Startup: How Today's Entrepreneurs Use Continuous Innovation to Create Radically Successful Businesses by Eric Ries

Likeable Social Media: How to Delight Your Customers, Create an Irresistible Brand, and Be Generally Amazing on Facebook by Dave Kerpen

Made to Stick: Why Some Ideas Survive and Others Die by Chip Heath and Dan Heath

Making Ideas Happen: Overcoming the Obstacles Between Vision and Reality by Scott Belsky

Never Eat Alone: And Other Secrets to Success, One Relationship at a Time by Keith Ferrazzi and Tahl Raz

Permission Marketing: Turning Strangers into Friends and Friends into Customers by Seth Godin

The Personal MBA: Master the Art of Business by Josh Kaufman

Pitch Anything: An Innovative Method for Presenting, Persuading, and Winning the Deal by Oren Klaff

Purple Cow: Transform Your Business by Being Remarkable by Seth Godin

Rework by Jason Fried and David Heinemeier Hansson

The Startup Playbook: Secrets of the Fastest-Growing Startups from Their Founding by David Kidder and Reid Hoffman

To Sell Is Human: The Surprising Truth About Moving Others by
Daniel Pink

*The War of Art: Break Through the Blocks and Win Your Inner Creative
Battles* by Steven Pressfield and Shawn Coyne

NOTES

Chapter 1

009. *When James Truslow Adams first put those two words together in 1931, Americans had yet to adopt prosperity as a core value . . .* From James T. Adams, *The Epic of America* (1931).

010. *Defined by the Small Business Administration as companies with fewer than 500 employees . . .* SBA Office of Advocacy, "Frequently Asked Questions," http://www.sba.gov/sites/default/files/sbfaq.pdf.

010. *According to a 2009 USA TODAY/Gallup Poll, roughly a quarter of working Americans have considered becoming an entrepreneur.* Laura Petrecca, "What Kind of Small Business Do You Want to Start?" *USA Today*, http://usatoday30.usatoday.com/money/small business/startup/pros-and-cons-of-small-businesses.htm.

012. *Half of all new companies fail within the first five years.* SBA Office of Advocacy, "Frequently Asked Questions," http://www.sba .gov/sites/default/files/sbfaq.pdf.

014. *A study done by the Kauffman Foundation—a renowned organization dedicated to promoting education and entrepreneurship—surveyed 549 company founders across various industries and found that more than half of the participants were first-generation entrepreneurs.* Numerous authors, "The Anatomy of an Entrepreneur," the Kauffman Foundation, http://www.kauffman.org/uploaded Files/ResearchAndPolicy/TheStudyOfEntrepreneurship/Anatomy %20of%20Entre%20071309_FINAL.pdf.

015. *The same Kauffman study from our first example found that 67 percent of the surveyed entrepreneurs ranked their academic*

performance among the top 30 percent of their undergraduate class. Ibid.

015. *Another study done by the Kauffman Foundation found that every year from 1996–2007, Americans between the ages of 55–65 had a higher rate of entrepreneurial activity than those aged 20–34, "averaging a rate of entrepreneurial activity roughly one-third larger than their younger counterparts."* Dane Stangler, "The Coming Entrepreneurship Boom," the Kauffman Foundation, http://www.kauffman.org/uploadedFiles/the-coming-entrepreneurial-boom.pdf.

015. *By 2011, the number had increased even more, with Americans between the ages of 55–64 making up 20.9 percent of all new entrepreneurs.* The Kauffman Foundation, http://www.kauffman.org/uploadedFiles/KIEA_2012_report.pdf.

016. *It's estimated that the average startup cost for a business is somewhere between $25,000-$50,000,* U.S Small Business Administration, "Frequently Asked Questions about Small Business Finance," http://www.sba.gov/sites/default/files/files/Finance%20FAQ%208-25-11%20FINAL%20for%20web.pdf

016. *Studies suggest that around 65% percent of entrepreneurs finance their companies using some form of personal debt.* U.S Small Business Administration, "How to Build Business Credit for Your Start Up," http://www.sba.gov/community/blogs/guest-blogs/industry-word/how-build-business-credit-your-start.

Chapter 2

021. *It's estimated that each day some 2,356 Americans become entrepreneurs.* Connor Boyack, *Latter-Day Responsibility: Choosing Liberty Through Personal Accountability,* (2012).

027. *"I am a huge believer that you go to college to learn how to learn,"* writes Mark Cuban on his blog. Mark Cuban, "Blog Maverick," http://blogmaverick.com/2012/05/13/the-coming-meltdown-in-college-education-why-the-economy-wont-get-better-any-time-soon/.

033. *When setting goals, you may find it helpful to use the SMART method, which was first developed by author George T. Doran in 1981.* George Doran, "There's a S.M.A.R.T. Way to Write Management's Goals and Objectives," *Management Review* 70, no.11 (November 1981).

Chapter 4

043. *It's estimated that a small business owner with less than one year of experience will earn as little as $34,000 a year.* K. J. Henderson, "The Average Income of Small Business Owners," http://smallbusiness.chron.com/average-income-small-business-owners-5189.html.

047. *A franchise is "a business system in which private entrepreneurs purchase the rights to open and run a location of a larger company.* Kristie Lorette, "Definition of a Franchise Business," *Houston Chronicle,* http://smallbusiness.chron.com/definition-franchise-business-4467.html.

050. *According to Ries, pivoting is a "structured course correction designed to test a new fundamental hypothesis about the product, strategy, and engine of growth.* The Lean Startup.com, http://theleanstartup.com/principles.

050. *Shortly after launching the app, CEO Brian Scordato noticed something interesting . . .* Brian Scordato, personal interview, April 5, 2013.

068. *With hundreds of thousand of trademarks registered each year . . .* The United States Patent and Trademark Office, Data Visualization Center, http://www.uspto.gov/dashboards/trademarks/main.dashxml.

075. *Business models can range in detail and complexity and intricacy, but a study done by the Massachusetts Institute of Technology Sloan School of Management in 2004 discovered that almost every model falls under one of four main archetypes.* Various authors, "Do Some Business Models Perform Better Than Others? A Study of the 1000 Largest US Firms," MIT Sloan, http://ccs.mit.edu/papers/pdf/wp226.pdf.

Chapter 5

078. *Cost-plus pricing . . .* Lisa Magloff, "What Is Cost-Plus Pricing Strategy?" *Houston Chronicle,* http://smallbusiness.chron.com/cost-plus-pricing-strategy-1110.html.

078. *Value-based pricing . . .* Craig Stedman, "Value-Based Pricing," *Computer World,* http://www.computerworld.com/s/article/42848/Value_Based_Pricing?amp;client=firefox-a&ct=clnk&cd=7&hl=en&gl=uk.

079. *Price-skimming . . .* "Price Skimming," Investopedia, http://www.investopedia.com/terms/p/priceskimming.asp.

079. *Penetration pricing . . .* Dana Griffin, "Penetration Pricing Strategy," *Houston Chronicle,* http://smallbusiness.chron.com/penetration-pricing-strategy-2723.html.

080. *Psychological pricing* . . . Farnoosh Torabi, "Pricing Psychology: 7 Sneaky Retail Tricks," *CBS Money Watch*, http://www.cbsnews .com/8301-505144_162-41541822/pricing-psychology-7-sneaky -retail-tricks/.

Chapter 6

092. *According to the United States government, a sole proprietorship, also referred to as a "sole trader" or "proprietorship," is an unincorporated business that is owned and run by one individual, with no distinction between the business and the owner.* U.S. Small Business Administration, "Sole Proprietorship," http://ccs.mit .edu/papers/pdf/wp226.pdf.

092. *Granted to an inventor by the United States government, a patent excludes others from "making, using, offering for sale, or selling the invention throughout the United States or importing the invention into the United States.* The United States Patent and Trademark Office, "Patents," http://www.uspto.gov/patents/.

092. *According to the United States Patent and Trademark office, the laws of nature, physical phenomena, and abstract ideas cannot be patented.* The United States Patent and Trademark Office, "Patentable Subject Matter—Living Subject Matter," http://www .uspto.gov/web/offices/pac/mpep/s2105.html.

092. *A trademark protects a brand, or more specifically, "a word, phrase, symbol, and/or design that identifies and distinguishes the source of the goods of one party from those of others.* The United States Patent and Trademark Office, "Trademark, Patent, or Copyright?" http://www.uspto.gov/trademarks/basics/definitions .jsp.

092. *According to US government, "works of authorship, such as writings, music, and works of art that have been tangibly ex- pressed.* Ibid.

093. *A 2010 survey by Travelers Insurance found that 94 percent of small-business owners feel confident* . . . Travelers Insurance, "Risk Management on Main Street," https://www.travelers.com/ about-us/travelers-institute/iw-documents/Risk-Management-on -Main-Street-For-Small-Business-Owners.pdf.

097. *Patents* . . . The United States Patent and Trademark Office, http:// www.uspto.gov/patents/.

Chapter 7

111. *According to the IRS, only "ordinary and necessary" expenses can be deducted from your business income, including such things as supplies, insurance, rent, and equipment.* Internal Revenue Service, "Deducting Business Expenses," http://www.irs.gov/Businesses /Small-Businesses-&-Self-Employed/Deducting-Business-Expenses.

111. *Below, however, you'll find a generalized breakdown of the type of taxes you can expect to pay.* Peri Pakroo, *The Small Business Start-Up Kit: A Step-by-Step Legal Guide* (2012).

136. *Diane Sawyer once said, "Great questions make great reporting."* Think Quest, "Interview with Diane Sawyer," http://library.think quest.org/18764/television/interview.html.

Chapter 9

144. *At one point in time, willpower was thought of as some mysterious, unquantifiable power that one either possessed or didn't. But that theory has since been disproven.* American Psychological Association, "What You Need to Know About Willpower," http:// www.apa.org/helpcenter/willpower.aspx.

Chapter 10

147. *According to the American Marketing Association, marketing is defined as "the activity, set of institutions, and processes for creating, communicating, delivering, and exchanging offerings that have value for customers, clients, partners, and society at large.* American Marketing Association, "Definition of Marketing," http://www.apa.org/helpcenter/willpower.aspx.

149. *Branding is "the practice of creating a name, symbol, or design that identifies and differentiates a product from other products.* Entrepreneur, "Branding," http://www.entrepreneur.com/encyclope-dia/branding.

150. *In 2012, Forbes magazine valued the Apple brand at $87.1 billion, up 52% from two years prior.* Kurt Badenhausen, "Apple Tops List of the World's Most Powerful Brands," *Forbes*, http://www .forbes.com/sites/kurtbadenhausen/2012/10/02/apple-tops-list-of -the-worlds-most-powerful-brands/.

154. *With more than 340 million tweets sent each day, and Facebook accounting for one out of every seven minutes spent online, finding a captive audience for your business isn't hard.* Shea Bennett, "100 Amazing Social Media Statistics, Facts and Figures,"

Media Bistro, http://www.mediabistro.com/alltwitter/100-social
-media-stats_b33696.

155. *According to industry experts, search engine optimization is a
"methodology of strategies, techniques, and tactics used to
increase the amount of visitors to a website by obtaining a
high-ranking placement in the search results page of a search
engine.* Webopedia, "Search Engine Optimization," http://www
.webopedia.com/TERM/S/SEO.html.

156. *Defined by the Content Marketing Institute as "the art of communicating with your customers and prospects without selling . . .*
Content Marketing Institute, "What Is Content Marketing?"
http://contentmarketinginstitute.com/what-is-content-marketing/.

158. *According to the Public Relations Society of America (PRSA),
public relations is a "strategic communication process that builds
mutually beneficial relationships between organizations and their
publics.* Public Relations Society of America, "What Is Public
Relations?" http://www.prsa.org/AboutPRSA/PublicRelations
Defined.

163. *With 56% of Americans on at least one social network . . .* Jay
Baer, "11 Shocking New Social Media Statistics in America,"
http://www.convinceandconvert.com/the-social-habit/11-shocking
-new-social-media-statistics-in-america/.

163. *Consider this: 91% of local searchers say they use Facebook to
find local businesses online and 71% of social media users say
they are more likely to purchase from a brand they are connected
with.* Nate Mendenhall, "6 Stats That Will Restore Your Faith in
Social Media," http://socialmediatoday.com/nate-mendenhall
/1437866/6-stats-will-restore-your-faith-social-media.

164. *With 23 percent of users checking their account at least five times
a day, and 47% of social network users saying Facebook has the
greatest impact on purchase . . .* Jay Baer, "11 Shocking New
Social Media Statistics in America," http://www.convincean
dconvert.com/the-social-habit/11-shocking-new-social-media
-statistics-in-america/.

164. *With over 100 million users, it's estimated that LinkedIn is 277%
more effective at generating business leads than other social
networks.* Cary Eridon, "11 LinkedIn Marketing Gems You're
Missing Out On," http://blog.hubspot.com/blog/tabid/6307/bid
/31374/11-LinkedIn-Marketing-Gems-You-re-Missing-Out-On.aspx.

Chapter 11

165. *Earl Tupper had a problem: his product wasn't selling.* PBS, "Biography: Earl Silas Tupper," http://www.pbs.org/wgbh/american experience/features/biography/tupperware-tupper/.

171. *Still, it's important to have a basic understanding of the general sales process, which can be broken down into seven major parts.* Rich, Spiro, and Stanton, *Management of a Sales Force*, 12th edition, page 66.

193. *An independent contractor is defined as "a person who contracts to do work for another person according to his or her own processes and methods* The Free Dictionary, http://legal-dictionary .thefreedictionary.com/Independent+Contractor.

193. *From design to support services, more than 17 million work as independent contractors each year—a number that's expected to hit 23 million by 2017.* MBO Partners, "The State of Independence in America," http://www.mbopartners.com/state-of-independence/docs /2012-MBO_Partners_State_of_Independence_Report.pdf.

Chapter 12

208. *Below you'll find seven of the most common leadership styles.* MindTools.com, "Leadership Styles," http://www.mindtools.com /pages/article/newLDR_84.htm,

Chapter 13

210. *First coined by Robert Greenleaf, this type of leadership is centered on helping others live up to their fullest potential.* Robert Green- leaf Center for Servant Leadership, "What Is Servant Leadership?" https://www.greenleaf.org/what-is-servant-leadership/.

Chapter 14

218. *The biggest challenge facing small businesses right now is that too many good, creditworthy borrowers still can't find the capital they need to grow and create jobs.* United States Small Business Admin- istration. "Strengthening the Lending Environment for America's Small Business," http://www.sba.gov/about-sba-services/7586/5779

222. *In total, those franchises accounted for $1.3 trillion in revenue and the creation of 7.9 million jobs.* United States Census Bureau, "Census Bureau's First Release of Comprehensive Franchise Data Shows Franchises Make Up More Than 10 Percent of Employer

Businesses," http://www.census.gov/newsroom/releases/archives
/economic_census/cb10-141.html

223. *Entrepreneur magazine's 2013 Franchise 500 list. Entrepreneur,*
"Entrepreneur 2013 Franchise 500," http://www.entrepreneur.com
/franchise500/index.html.

224. *According to the International Franchise Association, more than
40 of the 105 companies that began selling franchises in 2008 had
yet to report their first sale by the end of 2009.* Carol Tice,
"Franchise Your Business in 7 Steps," *Entrepreneur,* http://www
.entrepreneur.com/article/204998.

228. *According to the Business Reference Guide published by
Business Brokerage Press, the "rule of thumb" valuation for a
flower shop is 30–35% of annual sales + inventory, while the
valuation for a veterinary practice is 70% of annual revenues + inventory.* BizStats, "Valuation Rule of Thumb," http://
www.bizstats.com/reports/valuation-rule-thumb.php.

Talk the Talk: Small Business Terms to Know

Banner ads: http://www.pcmag.com/encyclopedia/term/38413/banner-ad.
Barriers to entry: http://www.investopedia.com/terms/b/barrierstoentry
.asp.
Capital: http://www.businessdictionary.com/definition/capital.html.
Cash flow: http://www.businessdictionary.com/definition/cash-flow.html.
Equity ownership: http://www.investorwords.com/1726/equity.html.
Franchisors: http://www.businessdictionary.com/definition/franchisor
.html.
Intellectual property: http://www.businessdictionary.com/definition
/intellectual-property.html.
Letter of intent: http://www.businessweek.com/small-business/legal
-forms/diyl-business- *Marketing:* http://www.investopedia.com/terms
/m/marketing.asp.
Market share: http://www.businessdictionary.com/definition/market
-share.html.
Proof of concept: http://www.businessdictionary.com/definition/proof-of
-concept.html. affairs/letter-of-intent-to-purchase-business.html.
Public relations: http://www.businessdictionary.com/definition/public
-relations.html.
Revenue: http://www.businessdictionary.com/definition/revenue.html.
Target market: http://www.entrepreneur.com/encyclopedia/target-market.
Turnkey operation: http://www.investorwords.com/5093/turnkey.html.

ABOUT THE AUTHOR

Michael Parrish DuDell is an author, speaker, and entrepreneur. Before founding his current company, race + vine, a marketing consulting firm, Michael was the editor of ecomagination.com—GE's cleantech and sustainable innovation website—and the host of ecomagination.com's web series *Green Room Live*. Prior to that, Michael served as managing editor of The Domino Project, a publishing company started by marketing guru Seth Godin and powered by Amazon.com. Michael has spoken for and consulted with companies ranging from startups to Fortune 500s, including such well-known organizations as American Express, L'Oreal, Kraft, Visa, and many more. He is a One Young World Ambassador, a member of the Young Entrepreneur Council, and an advisor to numerous companies, including the New York Tech MeetUp, the largest tech organization in New York. Learn more at MichaelParrishDuDell.com or on Twitter @notoriousMPD.